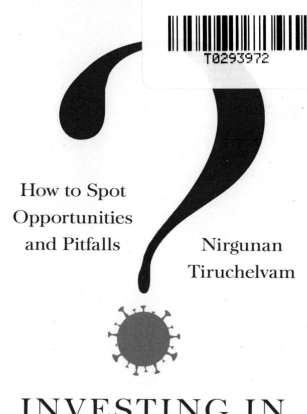

How to Spot
Opportunities
and Pitfalls

Nirgunan
Tiruchelvam

INVESTING IN
THE COVID ERA

mc Marshall Cavendish
Business

Articles were previously published in *The Edge Singapore*
© 2021 Nirgunan Tiruchelvam

Published in 2021 by Marshall Cavendish Business
An imprint of Marshall Cavendish International

A member of the
Times Publishing Group

Other Marshall Cavendish Offices:
Marshall Cavendish Corporation, 800 Westchester Ave, Suite N-641, Rye Brook,
NY 10573, USA • Marshall Cavendish International (Thailand) Co Ltd, 253 Asoke,
16th Floor, Sukhumvit 21 Road, Klongtoey Nua, Wattana, Bangkok 10110, Thailand
• Marshall Cavendish (Malaysia) Sdn Bhd, Times Subang, Lot 46, Subang Hi-Tech
Industrial Park, Batu Tiga, 40000 Shah Alam, Selangor Darul Ehsan, Malaysia

Marshall Cavendish is a registered trademark of Times Publishing Limited

National Library Board, Singapore Cataloguing in Publication Data

Names: Tiruchelvam, Nirgunan.
Title: Investing in the Covid era : how to spot opportunities and pitfalls / Nirgunan
Tiruchelvam.
Description: Singapore : Marshall Cavendish Business, 2021.
Identifiers: OCN 1232454737 | ISBN 978-981-4928-85-4 (paperback)
Subjects: LCSH: Investments—Singapore. | COVID-19 (Disease—Economic
aspects--Singapore.
Classification: DDC   332.6095957,dc23

Printed in Singapore

For Shehara, Antak and Vegav.

CONTENTS

Introduction

Equity analysts play the same role as movie critics. We recommend stocks for fund managers, just as critics guide cinema goers. Our views help direct investment. We are accredited gatekeepers.

The work involves sifting through thousands of pages of financial statements. It also requires computer modelling to create financial forecasts. Ultimately, the equity analyst needs to generate a report full of facts, figures and charts.

In my early days as an analyst, I used to travel the world to meet investors. This was before the COVID era when airports were functioning. I used to meet investors in financial centres like London, New York and Tokyo.

Once in Albuquerque, New Mexico, I was pitching the virtues of investing in rubber producers in Asia. The arid plains of New Mexico were a contrast from the greenery of tropical Asia. My enthusiasm for the investment theme and the boredom of the investors was an even sharper contrast.

I rattled off statistics on rubber demand and supply, but the investors dozed off. They were glancing at their Blackberries out of boredom. The minutiae of the figures made no impression. The end of my presentation came as a relief.

It was time to shift gear. I realized that it is better to pitch to the heart than the head.

The story of rubber became my pitch. Despite rubber being an old commodity, it is at the heart of industry. Without rubber, cars cannot operate. Rubber is vital for planes to land. It is the only way for rubber gloves and condoms to be manufactured.

Rubber was a wild crop in Brazil until the 1870s. It was domesticated by an English thief who took it to Malaya. Rubber can take up to 10 years to reach peak production. Hence, investors should pounce on the drop in rubber prices to buy rubber plantation stocks.

The investors were ecstatic. They promptly asked to meet the rubber companies. Before long, they were buying the stocks.

A successful pitch needs a narrative. The thoroughness of the analysis is irrelevant. People need to connect with your pitch with emotion.

This book seeks to popularize investing through stories. COVID-19 has devastated lives and companies. Investors need to come to grips with the catastrophe.

The immediacy of data in the digital age can mislead us. In October 1987, I was at an international boarding school in a remote hill station in South India. It was 14 hours from the nearest large city – Madras (now known as Chennai).

Bangalore, which is now the tech capital of Asia, was nine hours away. But in those days, Bangalore was more provincial than metropolitan. Its airport terminal was roughly the size of a large HDB.

The school followed the American curriculum and had students from over 35 countries. The library had glossy magazines like *Time, Newsweek* and *Sports Illustrated* that were then rare in India. India was an austere, isolated country that was following Soviet-style planning.

I used to follow the stock market closely. India's stock market was closed to foreigners, but I was transfixed by the gyrations on Wall Street. I had read a book called *The Confessions of a Stock Operator* by Edwin Lefevre. The book's protagonist is stock trader Jesse Livermore in the 1890s. He prospers by picking up the debris of a stock market collapse.

On 19 October 1987, the Dow Jones fell 23%. This catastrophe, named Black Monday, was a gilded opportunity to accumulate stocks. Within a week, the market had rallied 10%. But, *Newsweek*, *Time* and *The Wall Street Journal* arrived in my library two weeks after the collapse. The bird had flown.

News used to spread slowly in those days. India had only 30 minutes of English language programming a day. The state-owned TV station had a show called *The World this Week*. The buying opportunity passed by unnoticed.

Today, stock prices are instantly available. You can follow the markets on the Iphone in real-time. Trading is free.

But, investment research is not free of jargon. Terms like EBITDA, greenshoe, CBO, and CDO misguide more than inform. These terms can be simplified for both professionals and lay investors.

This book seeks to introduce investing in an accessible way. I use stories to convey complex concepts.

As Steve Lynch said, "If you're prepared to invest in a company, then you ought to be able to explain why, in simple language that a fifth grader could understand, and quickly enough so the fifth grader won't get bored."

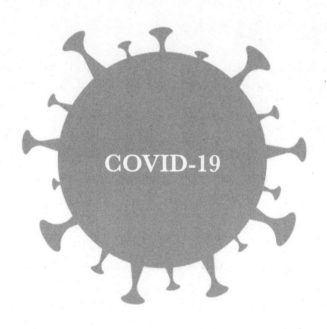

COVID-19

Sea in troubled waters

Published on October 09, 2020

In 1883, there was a circus pony called Dicky in Chicago. Dicky won the affection of the audience. He was skilful in jumping over a stack of books. The circus goers marvelled at his flexibility. Children laughed and clapped.

Dicky performed the same trick in the same circus for many years. The audience began to tire of this old trick. They soon realised that the pony could only perform one trick. The poor beast was eventually put to death.

Investors are raving at a one-trick pony today: **Sea**, a US-listed e-commerce and gaming company in this region. It has now become the best-performing stock in the world.

Sea has not got the attention of **Tesla** or the FAANGs. But, it has vastly outperformed those names. It has risen 750% in the last 18 months, including 416% in 2020 alone.

The loss-making company is not only the world's top performer, but now also the largest in Southeast Asia. At US$81 billion ($110 billion), its market capitalisation is more than those of Singaporean giants such as **DBS Group Holdings** and **CapitaLand**. It is even more than **BCA**, the Indonesian mega bank. At 30 times FY2019 revenue, it is more than eight times the average for its peers. Even a pony won't be able to scale its valuation.

Sea has two main lines of business—e-commerce and gaming. The e-commerce business is Shopee, a platform that Singaporeans have flocked to in COVID-19. Shopee commands a market share of 25% in the ASEAN e-commerce sector.

The problem is that Shopee is chronically cash-destructive. Sea's overall cash burn is dangerous. The Shopee losses could deplete its cash by FY2023.

Shopee received a spike in revenue due to COVID-19, which has forced people to buy even basic goods like groceries online. However, Shopee's COVID-19 spike is well below its peers in emerging markets. Even the spike has not halted the cash burn.

Sea's gaming business is called Garena. It is cash-flow positive and profitable. It could generate US$2 billion in revenue, which is a four-fold increase from three years ago.

However, it has an eerie similarity with Dicky, the pony that had only one trick. Garena is the only part of Sea's business that is operationally profitable. This is just an agency business. Most of the games are developed by others.

Also, the core of its gaming revenue comes from a single game—*Free Fire*, which is Sea's first self-made mobile game. It is in the Battle Royale category of games—games that simulate survival contests, like in the movie *Hunger Games*, where participants engage in a fight to the death.

Like Dicky's jump in the circus, *Free Fire* is now a phenomenally popular trick. It was the world's most downloaded game in 2019. *Free Fire* attracted more than 80 million daily active users in more than 130 markets.

But loyalty in gaming is fickle. Like fashion, adulation can turn to boredom. Investors in Sea are betting on a single game.

The man at the heart of this pony show is a soft-spoken engineer—Forrest Li. The 42-year-old Li was born in Tianjin, China. His rise has been stunning even by the standards of this era's tech billionaires.

He worked for the Chinese arms of US multinationals—**Motorola** and **Corning**. The turning point was when he got into Stanford MBA's program, the nursery of tech titans.

Li then followed his wife to Singapore, where she had a job, in 2006. He founded Garena (as Sea was then known) in 2009.

His big break was an early investment by the Kuok family. Sea was listed in 2017 with the backing of **Tencent**.

Li's immediate priority would be to generate cash. He should not rest on his skyrocketing stock price. Like circus-goers and gamers, investors are fickle. They may abandon the stock once the COVID-19 boost ends.

Sea's vast valuation cannot last indefinitely. As Forrest Gump, whose name Li adopted, said: "Life is like a box of chocolates. You never know what you're gonna get." That is a lesson that Dicky learnt and Li should heed.

Postscript

Sea Ltd has defied my scepticism. It has surged despite signs of a vaccine. In December 2020, it reached a valuation of US$100 billion, the first ASEAN company in that bracket.

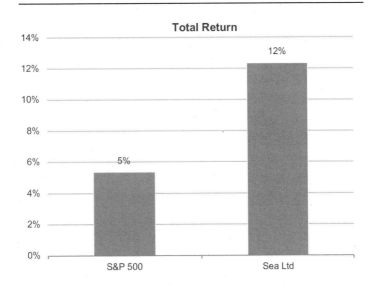

How to profit from a looming debt crisis

Published on September 28, 2020

Charles Dickens wrote *David Copperfield* in 1849, but its lessons remain vital. It features a clerk called Micawber, who lived beyond his means. He went to jail because he could not pay his debts. In those days, debtors could be jailed under English law.

Micawber is based on Dickens' own father, John Dickens. John had the gift of writing but had no money sense. He owed a baker GBP40, which is about $19.204 in today's money. John Dickens, the father of eight, was imprisoned with his four youngest children. Charles Dickens, who was then 12, had to seek work in a factory to bail out his old man.

Imprisoning debtors is still a common practice in the Gulf. Happily, debtors do not go to jail in England anymore. However, many may soon revisit the misery inflicted on the Dickens family. COVID-19 has not just claimed lives, but also millions of jobs. In many countries, including Singapore, job losses are mounting. In the US, unemployment is now at a 50-year high.

Joblessness is surging after a long consumer debt binge. US household debt hit a record US$13.7 trillion ($18.7 trillion) in 2019, which was around three quarters of GDP.

In the US, 68 million people had debt in collection on their credit report before COVID-19. That number will double by the end of 2020. Debt can be claimed by collectors after it is 180 days past due.

There is an industry that views bad debt as a godsend—debt collectors. This is an advanced industry. Though people associate debt collectors with loan sharks, it is a regulated business. Debt collectors play a vital function. If you cannot collect debts, the whole economy suffers.

Uncollected bad debts make it hard for legitimate borrowers to operate. Debt collectors are like plumbers. Their work can be dirty, but somebody has to drain the pipes of finance.

Opportunity lies in the highly advanced US debt collection industry. American debt collectors are governed by state and federal regulation. The debt collectors are barred from using threats of violence. They cannot shame debtors by publicising the issue. Instead, they collect by combining persuasion with threats.

Debt collectors make money in two ways. They could receive a fee from a creditor for collecting the money that is owed. For instance, let us assume a bank is owed a US$100 million in uncollected credit card debt. The debt collectors could get a fee of 5% of the face value for collecting it.

The second way that debt collectors make money is even more lucrative. The debt collector could buy the US$100 million debt from the bank. It could be bought at a discount of 20% to its face value—US$80m. They could then collect 90% of the face value of the debt. This would amount to a profit of US$10 million. The bank benefits because it means that the bad debt is off their books. The bank receives cash up front. It also saves the bank from the grind of chasing down debt. The last time that debt collectors had a bonanza like COVID-19 was in 2008–2010. The savage financial crisis put almost a tenth of the American workforce out of work. Also, the housing collapse meant that a fourth of sub-prime mortgages ended in foreclosure.

Debt collectors swept in on the bad debt like packs of hungry hyenas. Both the two major debt collectors listed in the US (**Encore Capital Group** and **PRA Group**) prospered.

PRA Group's net income doubled between FY08 and FY10. ,Its stock tripled over 24 months from its 2008 low. Encore, which was more aggressive in collection, saw its profits rise threefold over 2008–2010.

There are green shoots of a similar surge for these players in 2020. The lockdowns in the US provides them with a better chance of tracking down debtors. The stimulus package provides debtors with the means to trim their obligations. In 2Q2020, PRA Group said that cash collections rose 8% to record levels. At just 6x FY20 P/E, Encore stands out as a value play.

One man's misery is another man's fortune. The owners of jails prospered during the hardships of the Dickens era. As COVID-19 bites investors may want to back debt collectors.

Postscript

PRA has performed well on the back of recession concerns. Encore has underperformed, possibly due to its aggressive balance sheet.

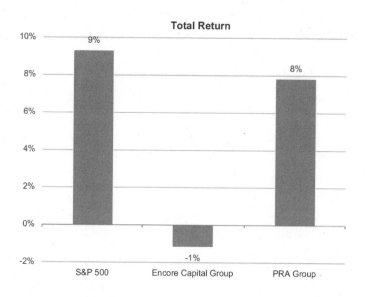

Beware the viral virus stocks

Published on May 22, 2020

In August 2005, Hurricane Katrina wiped out the American city of New Orleans. Nearly 2,000 people were killed and millions lost their homes.

The US government's response was as inept as the calamity was destructive. The dead were left unburied and the rescuers did not show up. Many condemned the George W. Bush administration's response as worse than that of a Third World country.

The fear of the natural disaster quickly led to stock market greed. A hurricane of a different kind drove up the stocks of hardware and construction companies. Home Depot, a seller of home appliances like tools and plumbing, rose sharply in the weeks after the disaster. Lowe's, another hardware chain, also rallied.

Construction stocks also gained from the new-found urge to rebuild. Granite Construction's stock rose 31% in the three months after Katrina. The company is a civil contractor and construction materials producer, specialising in public transportation infrastructure projects. Hurricane Katrina destroyed transport infrastructure in the American South but it was hoped that Granite could win construction contracts to rebuild the city.

However, the storm behind these stocks ended as suddenly as it emerged. Within a year of Katrina, these three stocks were below their pre-Katrina levels. The growth that the market was betting on proved to be elusive.

As with Katrina, COVID-19 has been a godsend for a new class of securities— the virus stocks which have prospered during the lockdown. These include video conference provider **Zoom** (up 155% ytd), online food ordering and delivery marketplace **GrubHub** (up 18% ytd) and exercise equipment and media company Peloton (up 58% ytd). These stocks are sitting ducks once the lockdown inevitably ends.

Zoom, which is headquartered in California, has gone viral. Its number of users have shot up 20-fold from just 10 million in December 2019 to above 200 million in April this year. Like Google and Xerox, Zoom now belongs to the magic circle of companies whose name is used as a verb.

But the skyrocketing usage figures seem misleading. The surge is mostly from free users who can host calls of up to 40 minutes. The customer growth from paid users, however, is much lower. The user experience has also dropped with the surge in free users, and the churn rates have risen recently.

There are also privacy and security issues, which could cause Zoom aversion for some users. Higher usage numbers also means more bandwidth investment. Its margins are stalling, as there are higher costs, without a corresponding rise in average revenue per user.

Though Zoom is trading at 2,100 times net profit in FY2020, there are many more "buy" recommendations than "sell". The street expects its net earnings to reach US$1 billion ($1.41 billion) by 2024. This would mean that its users need to triple to 750 million, assuming ARPU remains stagnant.

Investors are betting that Zoom's usage will expand due to an indefinite lockdown but this is a dangerous assumption. People may switch to rival video platforms like Facebook Messenger once Zoom's novelty evaporates and its flaws irritate users. Switching platforms is just as easy as signing up.

A similar stampede has greeted GrubHub, one of the largest food delivery platforms in the US. Like FoodPanda and Deliveroo in Singapore, GrubHub has become almost a necessity in the current COVID-19 lockdown. It has 110,000 restaurant partnerships in 2,000 American cities. GrubHub's usage has also doubled in the last year to almost 20 million.

Despite the massive surge in customers, GrubHub is on track to lose money in FY2020. If they cannot make money in lockdown, they may never turn a profit.

Operators like GrubHub have also adopted a predatory pricing policy by charging independent restaurants as much as 15% of an order, thus eating into their profits.

Though food delivery is touted as a tech business, it lacks the network effect. Unlike Uber which thrives with the expanding network of riders, food delivery companies are just body shops that cannot enjoy scale economics. A typical delivery person can only make about two deliveries per hour.

The street expects GrubHub's revenue to rise by a third by FY2022, but it still will not break even. It may be able to deliver food, but it will be a long time before it delivers profits.

Like hurricanes and viruses, investment fads are volatile. Investors who chase the fads could join the victims of these calamities.

Postscript

Zoom has continued to rise as COVID-19 rages. There are reports of Zoom fatigue that could weaken the stock if the vaccine restores normalcy.

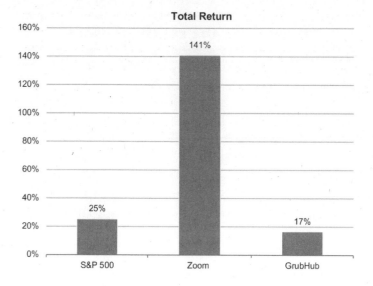

Total Return

Beware of the retail zombies

Published on May 8, 2020

In the movie *I am Legend*, Will Smith played the sole survivor in a pandemic. The post-apocalyptic thriller is set in a fictional New York City where a devastating virus wipes out most of humanity while turning a small percentage into violent mutants called darkseekers that were neither dead nor alive.

These darkseekers have superhuman survival skills and a lust for blood. Only sunlight can tame them. The movie was released in 2007 and is based on a 1954 novel, but it could also describe the troubled retailers in 2020.

JCPenney, a famous American department store chain founded in 1902, has fallen victim to the COVID-19 outbreak. It has closed 850 stores and furloughed thousands of workers to save cash. On May 4, this American retail titan—which survived wars, major recessions and the rise of online shopping—filed for bankruptcy.

But the chain's troubles preceded the virus and JCPenney has long suffered from a vile mix of financial leverage and operating leverage.

The store is one of many American retailers battered by online competition recently. Shoppers try out shoes, scarves and suits in the store. But, they then buy those items at a discount online.

Its long-term debt has also skyrocketed to US$4.6 billion ($6.5 billion). As a result, the net interest expense is US$300 million, which is hard to meet even before the lockdown.

Operational leverage is the degree to which operating income changes with revenue. JCPenney is vulnerable on this metric. Its ratio of fixed costs, such as staff and rent, to its total costs is high. In the last two years, revenue has fallen 14% but operating earnings have dropped twice as much.

Same store sales have fallen for the last two years. Many of the malls that housed the stores have also closed down.

The poor sales and heavy debt has bled the cash flow statement. At just US$386 million, its cash reserves are a fifth of the level in FY2015.

The lockdown also opened the doors of death for JCPenney: it had a US$105 million debt tranche maturing in June, which prompted the bankruptcy petition.

Other famous retailers such as **Neiman Marcus** and **Gap** are also on the brink. Neiman Marcus is desperately negotiating a haircut with lenders to cut its US$4.3 billion debt by half. Meanwhile, J.Crew—a one-time retail trendsetter—has also filed for bankruptcy.

Like the darkseekers, the dying retailers may have a magic potion that is more powerful than oxygen—bankruptcy laws and ultra-low interest rates.

Sears, a massive American department store that once owned the world's tallest building, went bust in 2018. However, about 400 of its stores are still functioning. Some of them have even opened their doors as the lockdown lifted in Georgia!

The Chapter 11 process in the US keeps businesses like Sears alive. It allows companies to continue while their debt is restructured. There is an "automatic stay" that restricts foreclosure and debt collection.

The other source of solace for the troubled retailers is the incredibly low interest rates. The COVID-19 crisis has merely further cemented these rates.

JCPenney was on its knees for several years. As recently as 2018, it raised US$400 million of debt at under 9%. This would not have been possible if not for the hunger for yield in a low interest rate environment.

A similar issue may arise in Asia, where retailers have been on a debt binge despite adversity. Over the last decade, the net leverage at listed Asian retailers has risen over threefold.

The Hong Kong-listed clothing retailer **Esprit Holdings** may face JCPenney's fate. Esprit is a producer of colourful sweatshirts that were once an aspirational item. Its sales rose 40-fold between 1993 and 2008.

In the last decade, Esprit has been outclassed by new retailers such as **Zara** as well as e-commerce. Its net debt is now twice its market capitalisation. Plus, the toxic combination of falling sales and soaring debt has driven the stock down 90% in the last five years. Last month, it shut all its stores outside China, its core market. The grim reaper is clearly not far. Chapter 11 is not known in Hong Kong and China but the region's complex bankruptcy laws allow the dead to survive.

Traditional retail is at death's door and COVID-19 may hasten the end. But, as with the darkseekers, a virus may not be the end.

Postscript
Traditional retailers like Gap have bounced back from the depths of the pandemic.

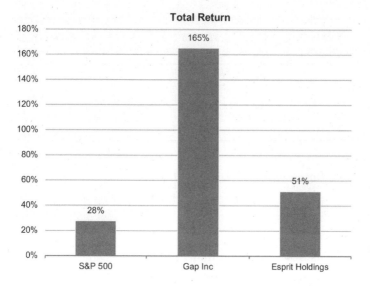

Total Return

S&P 500	28%
Gap Inc	165%
Esprit Holdings	51%

The big shorts in the COVID-19 crisis

Published on March 27, 2020

Michael Lewis's book *The Big Short* features a hedge fund manager called Michael Burry who profits from the 2008 crisis. Burry was deprived of sight in one eye at the age of two.

The boy with one eye viewed the world differently. He rarely made eye contact or socialised with others. Instead, he developed a passion for numbers. In 2007, he heavily shorted subprime mortgages and went on to make US$700 million as the market collapsed in 2008.

Today, short-sellers are among the few that have profited from the coronavirus collapse.

Short-sellers borrow shares and sell them hoping to buy them back at a lower price. They pocket the difference.

In the month ending March 19, shorts in the S&P500 and NASDAQ made US$344 billion ($501 billion). Both indices fell by a third in the period.

Hedge funds and private investors are now loading up their short positions. Many are looking to short the Asian markets, where shorting is banned by some regulators. The market collapse has prompted South Korea to ban short-selling for six months. In ASEAN, there are only two markets where short-selling is still unfettered—Singapore and Thailand.

There are three types of companies that are in the firing line, as we face an unprecedented shutdown across the region. Discerning investors with an eye on the bottom line should be alert to them.

First, companies with no inventory such as airlines, hotels, and cinemas, are weak.

Traditional businesses such as orange retailers carry inventory. If they hold an inventory of one million oranges and sales collapse for a month, they can sell it later. A hotel or an airline, on the other hand, has a finite number of room days or seats. If they do not operate for a month, then those room days or seats are gone forever.

There is no way that they can sell it, even at a discount.

Airlines such **Singapore Airlines** (down 23% year-to-date) and AirAsia (down 61% year-to-date) have all but ceased operations. The planes are grounded and they need to brace themselves for several months or quarters of cash burn. However, it may not be an ideal short at these levels. These airlines may have recourse to government bailout or support.

Second, companies with an operational crisis that have high fixed costs could suffer. **Village Roadshow** is an Australian cinema and theme park operator that may fit the bill. It operates the Golden Village chain of cinemas, as well as theme parks like Warner Bros and Sea World in Australia.

The fantasy theme parks are now turning into a nightmare. Village Roadshow has just announced that all its operations will cease. Australia has gone into an indefinite lockdown.

The trouble is that its net gearing level of 40% could be unsustainable. Two quarters of an operational standstill could cut its interest coverage ratio to below 1. Labour laws in Australia make it hard and expensive to fire workers. They could deplete its cash. There is a high chance that the 40% dividend payout rate could be cut, which may trigger a further fall.

A final category of shorts are companies that have exploded their debt before the crunch. **Minor International** is one of the largest hotel operators in Thailand. It is down 70% year-to-date. It has more than 12,800 rooms under brands such as Four Seasons, St Regis, and Marriott.

Minor International's problem is that it has nearly doubled its net gearing at precisely the wrong moment. In December 2018, it acquired the Spanish hotel operator NH Hotels Group for US$2.5 billion. The deal was financed by debt.

Minor International is bleeding from the collapse in hotel visitors. It needs to generate about US$120 million simply to maintain its interest obligations, while its hotels are empty. There are reports that its flagship Peninsular Hotel, a lavish property overlooking the Chao Phraya River, is operating at 5% occupancy. The European hotels are deserted. It could suffer a 80% fall in operating cash flow in FY2020.

Michael Burry's conviction that the US mortgage market would collapse was based on assiduous analysis. He saw with one eye what others could not see with two. The 2008 Lehman collapse vindicated him. Investors may want to keep an eye on Asian companies that are scarred by the virus.

Postscript

My fears that cinema operators, airlines and hotels would suffer in COVID-19 was vindicated. However, Village Roadshow and Minor International rose sharply from the lows of the crisis. SIA is still in the doldrums as the future of air travel remains bleak.

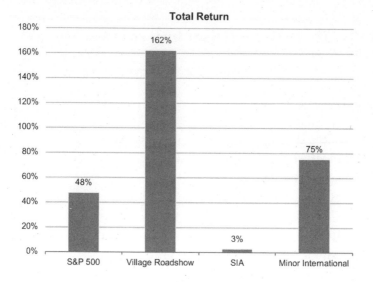

Is the coronavirus a bull market signal?

Published on March 13, 2020

COVID-19's impact has been brutal and sudden. The longest bull market has now suffered the fastest correction since the Great Depression.

However, investors in Singapore should take solace from a tragedy that occurred a hundred years ago. The Spanish Flu Pandemic of 1918 killed more people than World War I. Fifty million people died, according to some accounts, which was about 3% of the world's population then. It spread like wildfire infecting one in four humans—a total of 500 million people.

British Malaya, which included Singapore, suffered immensely. The territory was a vital source of rubber and tin for the British Empire. It was closely integrated commercially and militarily to the rest of the world.

About 1% of British Malaya's population of 3.6 million perished, according to a paper by Dr Kai Khiun Liew of Nanyang Technological University. However, the death rate in other parts of the world was much worse. It was more than 4% in some parts of India, where the flu killed seven million people.

Back then, the virus seemed to have entered the territory through the port of Singapore. Travellers used to dock from as far afield as Vladivostok (in today's Russia), which was heavily afflicted.

Those who are panicking today should consider the following. Health standards are infinitely better nowadays. Singaporeans now have access to antibiotics and world-class healthcare facilities. In 1918, the hospitals were unable to cope. Infected patients had to sleep along the corridors.

Medical staff themselves were infected, as this was long before health warnings. Thousands were infected by gathering in public places. On Nov 13, massive crowds gathered to celebrate the end of the war on Nov 11. The warnings to avoid large gatherings were completely ineffective.

Many cinema owners and mall operators in Singapore are now complaining bitterly about the poor footfall due to COVID-19. This is trivial compared to the devastation that the Spanish Flu brought: from September 1918 to the end of the year, up to 50 people were dying every day in Singapore. The situation was worse elsewhere in Malaya. But business continued unabated. Singapore traded heavily with the rest of the world. It was the epicentre of the world's rubber trade, because the London auction had closed due to World War I. Almost one-third of the world's rubber was exported from Singapore, compared to less than 5% in 1914. Singapore was directly exporting Malayan rubber to the US, bypassing London.

The year of such death was a bountiful period for commerce.

At the end of the war in 1918, people flocked to Paris Cinema on Victoria Street to watch silent newsreels of the victory. Talking movies were some years in the future.

Entertainment was undiminished elsewhere. In London, the Palladium Theatre in London had a germ-killing spray to assuage fear. This theatre continues to survive and thrive up till today.

The stock markets rose in spite of the pandemic. After the US entered the war in 1917, economic activity picked up. It became a workshop of the world. When the war ended at the end of 1918, the demilitarisation of soldiers back to civilian life caused a brief economic slowdown. In addition, the US suffered heavy casualties due to the flu, but the impact on commerce was comparatively muted.

In 1918, the stock market's return was higher than the long-term average: the Dow Jones Industrial Average (Dow) rose 11% that year, including reinvested dividends.

The Dow components then included some counters that are still thriving—General Electric, US Steel and Western Union. Other companies such as Utah Copper and Westinghouse have merged into Chevron Corp and Rio Tinto.

The world is much more integrated today. Disease can spread much quicker in the jet age. Population density is maybe fourfold higher today. We are much more vulnerable to fear and panic due to instant communication; the Spanish Flu occurred long before the Twitter age.

Nonetheless, stock markets and commerce rose in the face of death a century ago. The pall of gloom may lift sooner than the doomsayers expect. The savage correction that we suffered this past week may be overdone.

Postscript

The depths COVID-19 was a gilded opportunity to accumulate. The S&P500 rose by more than a third.

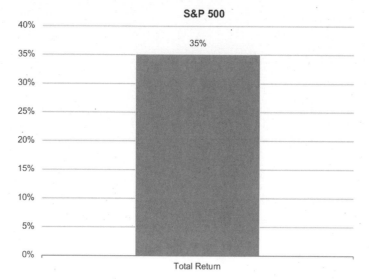

BUSINESS
PRACTICES

Why the VIX might do the trick

Published on November 9, 2020

Alfred E. Neuman was a fictional character in *Mad* magazine. He was cross-eyed, gap-toothed and always smiling. Neuman was never bothered by any setback.

Neuman's motto "What, me worry?" could be the catchphrase of the equity market. The market has greeted the election un-certainty with glee. Technology stocks have powered yesterday's rally. The NASDAQ 100 is up 4%, while the S&P500 rose 2%. Even the suspension of Ant Group Co's IPO was brushed aside.

However, a tortured battle looms. As Joe Biden closes in on victory, President Trump has vowed to fight to the finish. The relentless Trump has already petitioned the courts. There may not be a resolution before the inauguration, which is 76 days away.

The chaos could wipe the smile off Neuman's face. It could also wipe out the S&P500 gains. There is a distinct possibility of violence. Come January 20, Trump may not vacate the White House, even after Biden has been sworn in. The use of force may end the impasse.

The last time that there were fears of violence in an election dispute was in 1876. The popular vote was won by the Democratic candidate Samuel Tilden, but his Republican opponent Rutherford Hayes claimed victory in the electoral college. Hayes claimed 20 electoral college votes, which Tilden disputed.

In those days, the gap between election and inauguration was four months. A crisis crippled commerce. The stock market sank sharply as war fears rose. Investors hoarded gold and silver, which are now known as risk assets.

The matter was finally resolved in Hayes' favour on March 5, 1877. The clincher was the outgoing President Ulysses Grant's threat to forcibly prevent Tilden's inauguration.

The situation is even more dangerous today. Unlike Grant, the sitting President Trump is not a neutral arbiter, but the chief player in the dispute. As the commander-in-chief, there are plausible scenarios that could end in bloodshed.

Finance has progressed since 1876. Investors during uncertainty have more options than hoarding jewellery.

One striking innovation is the **VIX Index**, also known as the fear gauge. The VIX measures the market's expectation of 30-day, forward-looking volatility. The volatility is implied by the prices of S&P options.

The Index has its origins in the work of two finance professors Dan Galai and Menachem Brenner, who wrote about it in 1989. This inspired the Chicago Board Options Exchange (CBOE) to create the VIX Index.

Typically, the VIX Index spikes when the S&P500 declines sharply. In bull markets, the VIX drops steadily. When the market collapsed from February 27 to March 18, the VIX rose fourfold. On March 18, many index stocks like **Facebook** and **Apple** hit their one-year lows. Today, the VIX is hovering at a 65% discount to its March high.

The direction of a market is hard to predict. However, the VIX is a rough proxy for fear. There are VIX ETFs to help players to profit from rises in the expected volatility of the S&P500. These include ProShares Ultra VIX Short-term Futures ETF and Lyxor S&P 500 VIX Futures Enhanced REIT. There are also VIX indices that track assets ranging from commodities to currencies. Trading volatility has become one of the most popular ETFs in 2020. This year more than

US$1.5 trillion ($2 trillion) derivative bets were made. This is five times the figure in 2010, according to the CBOE.

The VIX Index has inadequacies as a hedge. It only measures 30 days of implied volatility. It does not always rise with a sell-off. For instance, it fell during the September sell-off. Also, it rolls over after a spike in volatility. It's not like holding a stock.

Investing in solid consumer names could serve as a hedge. For instance, the highly branded consumer giants like **Nestle** and **Unilever** sell essential items such as groceries and personal care. Their brands include household names like Lux, Kit Kat and Rinso. Their earnings have been resilient in the COVID-19 carnage. At a dividend yield of 3%, they seem enticing.

Other traditional stocks that could weather the storm include **Campbell Soup**. The US giant was one of the few consumer names that prospered in 2008, as soup was viewed as a comfort food. However, investors will need more than soup if the election defies resolution. Even Alfred E. Neuman's smile may turn to a frown.

Postscript

The US election results were not accepted by Trump. However, his legal challenges were unsuccessful. A transition to Biden has begun. Volatility did not spike.

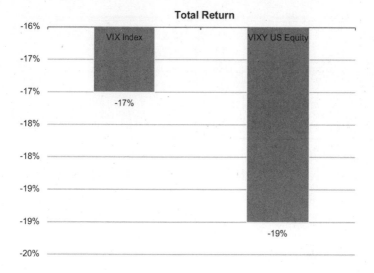

Total Return

VIX Index   -17%

VIXY US Equity   -19%

Donald Trump is a godsend for US banks

Published on December 5, 2016

Donald Trump's shock victory has led to irate protest marches. Wall Street bankers were not among those holding placards.

The president-elect's promise to repeal the onerous Dodd-Frank Act is music to the ears of beleaguered bankers. The Dodd-Frank Act was passed in the wake of the global financial crisis (GFC) of 2008.

It was the most radical piece of financial regulation since the 1930s. President Barack Obama hoped the legislation would "lift our economy". The Act, which runs into thousands of pages, vowed to "end too big to fail" and "promote financial stability".

Dodd-Frank was driven by the canard that the financial crisis was a result of deregulation. Actually, regulation of financial services expanded every year from 1999 to 2008. GFC was not due to deregulation but poor regulation.

The US government's affordable housing policy led to a weakening of underwriting standards. Lenders took on homes that they could not afford. The Federal Reserve fuelled the bubble by suppressing interest rates. Inflated housing prices caused an immense strain on the world's financial system.

Dodd-Frank has been a millstone around the neck of the financial sector. It has harmed not just Wall Street, but Main Street as well. The most draconian part of the Act was the "Volcker rule", which bars banks from proprietary trading in the stock and bond markets.

By restricting banks from proprietary trading, the Act has damaged the corporate bond market. Liquidity in the world's corporate bond markets has fallen by a fifth in the last five years. The evaporation of liquidity worsens risk. Markets are now more vulnerable than during the height of GFC.

Another outrageous feature of Dodd-Frank was the enthronement of bureaucrats. It created the Consumer Financial Protection Bureau. The director of this agency can outlaw any consumer credit product, and CFPB can override Congress and the courts. This has had a severe impact on consumer lending in the US, where recovery from GFC has been tepid.

The Act has made the Fed effectively board members of every large financial institution. The Fed has "heightened prudential supervision" over large banks. This provision can extend to asset management, insurance companies and even conglomerates such as GE.

The upshot of Dodd-Frank is the heavy cost of compliance. Banks have had to hire more personnel to grapple with the red tape and they are constrained from lending. This has throttled US recovery and, by extension, the world economy.

It has also made the big banks bigger and driven small banks into oblivion. The number of banks with an asset base of less than US$50 billion has fallen sharply by a fourth, removing a valuable source of credit.

In the wake of Trump's win, US bank stocks have surged. The **Financial Select Sector SPDR** exchange-traded fund has rallied more than 10% since Aug 9. The rally has been supported by the surge in bond yields. **JP Morgan Chase & Co.**, one of the largest components of the ETF, has hit all-time highs. **Goldman Sachs Group** and **Bank of America** are up 14%.

This may be only the beginning of a sustained rally. Several US banks stocks are trading at a 40% discount to their tangible book value. This is almost two standard deviations from the mean over the last quarter century.

On price-to-earnings multiples, they are dirt cheap. The valuations of the major US banks are at just 12 times forward earnings, compared with 18 times for the Standard & Poor's 500 index. This is well below the peak valuation of 33 times that was achieved in May 2009 before the jackboot of regulation was imposed.

The repeal of Dodd-Frank is one of several triggers for unlocking value. Trump's win may also lead to inflation. He plans to widen the fiscal deficit with a massive infrastructure programme. The yield on 10-year Treasury has risen 25% since his win and the yield spread has widened. This has improved the earnings prospects of banks.

The rosy outlook for banks should not obscure the risks. Dismantling the regulations will take several months of tortured negotiations. Trump will have to contend with the interest groups that are surviving like leaches on the largesse of Dodd-Frank.

As his unexpected win shows, Trump can defy the odds. US banks may be about to rise from a seven year rout on the shoulders of a reality-TV star.

Postscript

Trump's measures to free the banking industry of regulation have been a boon for the sector. The stocks have rallied, but not as well as the market.

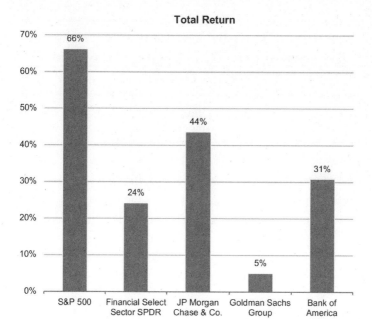

Total Return

S&P 500	66%
Financial Select Sector SPDR	24%
JP Morgan Chase & Co.	44%
Goldman Sachs Group	5%
Bank of America	31%

'President Trump' could boost prospects for corporates like Apple, Cemex and Geo Group

Published on January 18, 2016

In 1927, Charles Lindbergh became the first person to fly across the Atlantic. The 25-year-old's flight from New York to Paris took 33 hours, but his fame lasted much longer. The lanky and elegant pilot was feted to the heavens. Over 100,000 people greeted him in a ticker tape parade on his return to New York.

Lindbergh's prestige sank when he became a Nazi sympathiser in the late 1930s. An admirer of Adolf Hitler, he was opposed to the US entering World War II. He blamed the Jews for pushing the country into the conflict.

A decade ago, Philip Roth wrote *The Plot against America*, a work of alternative history. In this novel, Lindbergh defeats Frederick Roosevelt in the 1940 presidential polls. Lindbergh makes a peace pact with Hitler and imposes severe anti-Semitic policies. For instance, Jewish youth are sent to the South and Midwest to be "Americanised". Jewish immigration is barred, and vicious violence is orchestrated.

Reality seems to be blending with fiction in the current US presidential elections. Donald Trump, the flamboyant businessman vying for the Republican ticket, has vowed to impose a "total lockdown" on Muslim visitors to the US. He also wants to build a wall to keep Mexicans from getting into the US and conduct a mass deportation of 11 million illegal aliens.

Under Trump, the US would pursue an isolationist foreign policy. Trump points out that the country has spent some US$4 trillion ($5.7 trillion) on wars since 2001 and argues that the money would have been better spent on infrastructure and healthcare at home. He also does not want to see any company pay more than 15% of its business income in taxes.

Trump appears to have struck a chord with both Wall Street and the man on the street. A Trump presidency now seems a distinct possibility. How should investors position themselves for Trump in the White House?

A crackdown on illegal immigrants would be disastrous for the economy, as it would be inflationary. However, there are companies that would gain from Trump's jackboot. These include private prisons and security firms. The US has the highest rate of incarceration in the world and the government prison system would not be able to accommodate the mass arrests and deportation.

The **Geo Group** is a private prison real estate trust and the largest provider of detention services in the US. It has longstanding contracts with US Immigration and Customs Enforcement (ICE). The federal government accounts for nearly half of Geo's revenue, with ICE alone representing a sixth of that.

In 2013, the government revealed that undocumented aliens were detained at an average of 34 days at the cost of US$120 a day per bed. Geo provides these beds. If Trump were to make good on his promise to boot all illegal aliens out of the US, some 11 million people would have to face the judicial process before they are actually deported.

This could boost Geo's revenue and earnings. Illegal aliens would not be all that is repatriated by "President Trump". Under his flat 15% tax rate, companies would not be able to defer taxes on overseas income. Foreign tax credit would ensure that companies avoid double taxation. Trump would create a repatriation tax holiday of 10%. US corporations are stashing US$2.1 trillion of cash overseas, amounting to a seventh of the country's GDP. Much of the cash mountain is held by the tech giants such as Google, Apple, Facebook and Amazon.com.

Apple has an estimated US$150 billion of cash reserves overseas, which is about 92% of its total reserves. The income tax cut from 35% to 15% would be a godsend to Apple. It would effectively increase the net profit margin of the world's largest corporation by 31%.

As for Trump's proposal to build a 1,000-mile-long wall along the US-Mexico border, the obvious beneficiaries would be suppliers of building materials. The wall could cost up to US$25 billion, at least a fourth of which would be for cement. With Trump's claim that he will force the Mexican government to fund the wall, shares in US-listed cement company **Cemex** are enticing. The company has a large presence in Mexico.

The real-life Lindbergh was more of an enigma than a hero. Over a quarter century after his death, it was discovered that he had fathered seven children out of wedlock by three women in Europe. Though Trump's agenda may have its own skeletons in the closet, it would be a presidency like no other.

Postscript

Trump defied all odds and won the Presidency in November 2016. I was vindicated. The S&P500 nearly doubled. Apple has risen more than fourfold. Cedex and Geo have performed but not as brightly.

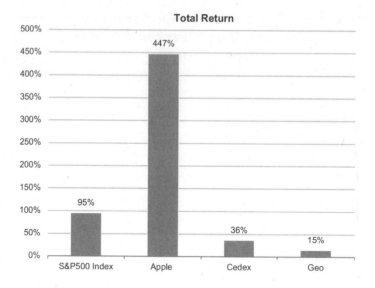

Total Return

- S&P500 Index: 95%
- Apple: 447%
- Cedex: 36%
- Geo: 15%

Lessons from Bernie Ebbers' acquisitions spree

Published on February 14, 2020

The former WorldCom CEO Bernie Ebbers, who died at the age of 78 this month, started life as a basketball coach. He often urged his employees to act in concert like a baseball team.

But, Ebbers' memory will ring loud for a different reason. WorldCom, a telecom giant, was one of the spectacular casualties of the dotcom collapse of 2000. It was once the only company that could connect long-distance calls throughout the US. Its market capitalisation peaked at US$185 billion, or US$272 billion ($377 billion) in today's terms. This is more than the valuation of any telco today.

Ebbers, who stood at six foot five and weighed 200 pounds, bullied his employees. But, he had a charming demeanour with investors. He captivated Wall Street with his vision of dominance of the booming telco landscape.

WorldCom's dazzling rise under Ebbers was built on two pillars—acquisitions and earnings growth. It grew by gobbling up over 75 companies. In 1998, Ebbers' purchase of MCI for US$47 billion made it second only to **AT&T** in the US telco field.

Earnings growth was squeezed out of the acquisitions through cost-cutting and aggressive accounting. The market was fixated on the ever-increasing EPS numbers. He slashed thousands of jobs and even banned free coffee in an effort to hit the earnings growth target.

The music eventually stopped. WorldCom's undoing was its foray into fibre optics at the turn of the century. The fibre optics industry was viewed as the magic platform for the growth of the internet. WorldCom overstretched itself by excessive investment in fibre optics. The dotcom collapse in 2000 paralyzed the sector and exposed WorldCom's frailties.

Within a year, the stock lost almost 90% of its value. WorldCom had accumulated US$30 billion in net debt from its buying spree. Crucially, the mood had turned hostile towards fibre optics. The streets were littered with insolvent tech companies.

The spotlight turned on Ebbers. It turned out that WorldCom had loaned him $408 million to buy stock. It was found that he had improperly exaggerated profits by treating operating expenses as capital expenditure.

Ebbers was eventually sentenced to 25 years in prison in 2015 for 11 counts of accounting fraud – the largest white collar conviction.

Asia is in a similar position to the US in the 1990s. There is a massive capital expenditure boom in the telco sector, as 5G looms.

In the 1990s, the US was the centre of the telco boom. Today, the world's leaders in the field are Huawei, **Xiaomi** and **Samsung**, which are in Asia. The low interest rates have spurned a debt binge. The boom is funded by the largesse of the banks. In ASEAN alone, net debt levels have nearly doubled in the last decade.

There are some traps that Asian investors should be alert to.°

First, acquisitive companies could be dangerous investments. Once WorldCom acquired a company, the principal focus was to cut the costs to provide a post-facto justification for the deal. Half of the headcount was axed in several cases.

WorldCom was a roll-up, which is a company that adds value by acquisition. A roll-up company is risky, because the expectation of further success rises with every deal.

Second, complicated accounting practices could be designed to mislead investors. WorldCom aggressively treated operating expenses as capital expenditure to exaggerate its earnings. Capital expenditure is typically deducted from earnings in small chunks.

Third, inflated balance sheets can be problematic when the market turns. After the dotcom collapse, WorldCom had US$30 billion in debt, which was more than twice its market cap.

Wilmar International, a commodity trader, is one of the region's most indebted. It is carrying US$18 billion of net debt, after spending about US$5 billion in capex in the last five years. The market is ignoring its leverage risk, because its net interest rate is only 2%. This comfortable cost of funding may not be sustainable if the exchange rates move against them.

Ebbers' lawyers pleaded his innocence by citing his poor grasp of finance. They stressed his roots as a basketball coach, where he often yelled at his players to keep their eyes on the ball. But investors in Asia's high growth companies should instead keep their eyes out for accounting tricks.

Postscript

There is increased scrutiny on aggressive accounting. It is likely that some of Asia's high growth stocks may fall victim to accounting fraud.

Are roll-ups brewing in beer and coffee?

Published on June 5, 2020

In the 1988 Seoul Olympics, Canadian sprinter Ben Johnson smashed the world record for the 100-metre dash. He leapt to the finish line in just 9.79 seconds, a timing that was then scarcely believable. His competitors included Olympic champions Carl Lewis and Linford Christie, who were blown away.

Johnson was feted as a god-like figure. The photo of his muscular frame crossing the finishing line was on every front page. He told reporters that his record would last 100 years.

However, within days of the race, joy turned to dismay. To the shock of his supporters, Johnson had failed a drug test. A performance-enhancing substance called stanozolol was found in his urine. Stanozolol helps athletes get stronger and build muscle mass.

Johnson was stripped of his medal and record. He has lived in disgrace since.

In the pharmaceutical industry, Johnson's rise and fall was mirrored by Valeant Pharmaceuticals. The Canadian company, which was valued at US$86 billion at its peak, was led by Michael Pearson, a former McKinsey consultant.

Like Johnson, Pearson was ahead of his peers in the industry. Valeant's stock rose 40-fold during Pearson's eight-year tenure that began in 2008. Its operating profits grew 10-fold.

Pearson expanded Valeant by acquiring smaller pharmaceutical companies and cutting costs. The deals were financed by debt.

In August 2005, Valeant's frailties were exposed. It was revealed that Valeant had an improper relationship with a mail-order drug company called Philidor. Philidor was pricing its drugs well beyond the means of consumers. This led to investors zooming in on Valeant's vulnerabilities.

Valeant was a blatant example of a roll-up company — a company that creates growth by acquisition. Growth by debt-financed acquisition was Valeant's drug. Like what stanozolol did for Johnson, it made Valeant appear invincible.

Investing in a roll-up oriented company is risky. The more successful an acquisition, the higher the market's expectations of the next one. There is an insatiable need to feed the beast.

Once an acquisition disappoints, the precipice looms. Valeant had US$30 billion in debt by 2016, which was three times its sales—a dangerous position. The stock lost 91% of its value in the year prior to March 2016. Pearson's career ended in disgrace.

Today, there are two roll-up companies that are feted, although they carry serious risks. They both produce beverages that provide comfort—beer and coffee.

AB InBev could lay claim to be the Valeant of beer. The multinational company, which listed its Asian arm (Budweiser APAC) in Hong Kong last year, produces more than 50 beer brands. These include Budweiser, Stella Artois and Corona. One out of every four beers in the world is produced by AB InBev.

It seems to have an ominous similarity to Valeant Pharmaceuticals. Its growth strategy is built on acquiring rivals. In 2017, AB InBev bought its main rival SABMiller for US$103 billion to cement its grip on the beer market.

It then raised the price of beer. Budweiser APAC's growth is dependent on premiumisation—the practice of introducing higher-priced beers. Valeant was bent on increasing the price of its drugs after acquiring smaller rivals.

Beer consumption is flat in rich countries and falling in emerging markets. Young people are spending more time in gyms than in bars in the West. If the acquisitions are taken out of consideration, AB InBev has not raised beer volumes in the past decade.

Last week, the drowsy IPO market received a shot of espresso. **JDE Peet**'s, the world's second-largest consumer coffee company, listed in Amsterdam and raised US$2.5 billion ($3.5 billion). This is the first major listing in the COVID-19 era.

However, investors should gulp down a stiff cup of coffee rather than a glass of champagne. The growth of JDE Peet's seems to be driven by deals and not organic growth. It could be the roll-up of coffee.

JDE Peet's controls brands such as Douwe Egberts, Kenco and Peet's Coffee. It has acquired famous local brands such as Old Town and Super Group. Its real EBITDA growth in FY17–19 is more modest than the headline CAGR of 10%. That may not be growth levels that deserve 17x EV/ EBITDA in the middle of a pandemic.

As the Seoul Games have shown, those who win the race may not retain the title.

Postscript

The two roll-up companies (JDE Peet's and AB InBev) have had contrasting fortunes. The market seems wary of JDE Peet's acquisitions. AB InBev has risen due to a belief that it would prosper as lockdowns ease.

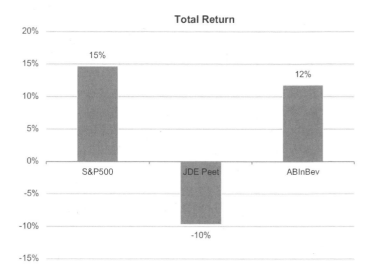

Total Return

Luckin Coffee: Why did investors ignore the red flags?

Published on April 24, 2020

Ivar Kreuger, dubbed the Match King, used to kiss women on the wrist when introduced, and not on the hand. He was afraid of germs.

A man of piercing intellect, he helped pioneer safety matches—then used for lighting everything from stoves to cigarettes. His companies produced almost three quarters of the world's matches.

But Kreuger was also a swindler. His empire was built on fictitious sales, which collapsed in the wake of the Great Depression, leading to his suicide in 1932. It was said that he burned through—in today's money—US$1.5 billion ($2.14 billion) of financier's funds.

Almost a century after his death, Kreuger's legacy lives on: not because of his aversion to germs before the COVID-19 era, but due to his use of accounting tricks.

Luckin Coffee—China's answer to global chain Starbucks —may be one of Kreuger's inheritors. It has been allegedly cooking the books instead of just brewing the coffee.

On April 2, the company revealed that its chief operating officer Liu Jian may have faked RMB2.2 billion ($445.04 million) of sales in FY2019. The amount represents almost half of the projected FY2019 revenue of US$732 million. Liu—who has been with the company since 2018—was suspended pending an investigation.

The stock sank 81% on April 3 and has lost more than 90% of its value since its May 2019 IPO. Muddy Waters, a short seller led by Carson Block, had announced it was shorting the stock after an anonymous report in January. Luckin Coffee's angry denial earlier has now come back to haunt it.

Chairman Charles Lu Zhengyao and CEO Jenny Qian Zhiya have defaulted on the US$518 million margin loan. Their shares have been handed over to the banks.

Luckin Coffee was founded in October 2017 in Xiamen. It rose at breakneck speed from a startup to a NASDAQ listing in just 18 months, backed by shareholders including GIC and BlackRock. Its revenue was projected to grow sixfold Y-O-Y in FY2019. Its 4,500 outlets exceed that of Starbucks in China. It also raised US$645 million in its IPO.

In its listing, Luckin Coffee's management—projecting a Kreuger-esque confidence—presented itself as a rival to Starbucks, where the average cup of coffee was sold at about a third cheaper. But coffee was sold not through a transaction with a cashier who doubles as a barista. Instead, the purchase would be through an app and delivered through cheap delivery platforms.

Luckin Coffee also avoided the fancy furniture and large floor space of its major rivals. In fact, its outlets were basically holes in the wall slightly larger than a teh tarek (pulled tea) shop. Customers were wooed by coupons and what was touted as premium Arabica coffee.

The chain's rapid revenue growth drove a sea of red through its income statement and cash flow statement. In FY2018, its losses were 1.5 times more than its revenue. In a perverse twist, this cash burn actually increased its merits in the heady summer of 2019. Investors were willing to tolerate and fund the cash burn, as long as a path to profits was remotely discernible.

Apart from its extremely short operating history, there were glaring red flags. The management had sold 49% of their stock holdings through pledges. This eventually magnified the sell-off through margin calls.

The company announced store-level profitability in 3Q2019. This meant that it was profitable excluding operating expenses and other charges. However, the latest revelations suggests that sales have been fabricated to satisfy this yardstick. Its net selling price was inflated, according to the anonymous short selling report.

The final source of suspicion could be the need to raise funds without a discernible purpose, except to bridge the cash burn. Just before the COVID-19 carnage, it raised another US$865 million via a convertible bond issue and share sale.

The combination of growth fuelled by a cash burn and a massive share pledge was an unpalatable brew. We may have entered a bear market, when the scandals are exposed. Cooking the books can be as destructive as any kind of disease. Caution would serve investors well, just like Kreuger's wariness of germs.

Postscript
Luckin Coffee's frailties were exposed by COVID-19. It remains a poster child for accounting fraud.

What are the lessons from the Hyflux haircut?

Published on December 20, 2019

In the 1970s, long-haired visitors to Singapore were required to cut their hair on arrival as unkempt locks were linked to hippie culture.

Investors in Singapore are now pondering a haircut of a different kind. Hyflux, once a marquee water treatment company, struggled to pay its debts after entering the power supply business. It has since been desperately seeking a white knight. A total of 34,000 retail investors in Hyflux's preferred debt were left in the lurch. The situation even prompted a public protest.

Utico has offered $300 million for a 95% stake in Hyflux. It will provide $100 million in working capital. The UAE company has offered Hyflux's unsecured debt holders a haircut of 50% on the par value of its debt. Hyflux's equity investors are facing a haircut of 90%, as it is valued at $16 million, according to the terms. The company had a market capitalisation of more than $165 million before its suspension in March 2018.

Utico's deal is the second prominent rescue operation of an embattled SGX firm by a UAE-owned investor. In 2017, Abu Dhabi Financial Group (ADFG), controlled by Jassim Alseddiqi, took an 8% stake in Noble Group Holdings, which was then one of Asia's largest commodity traders. Noble had lost more than half its value after an attack by a short seller.

ADFG's investment seemed a judicious move as Noble was trading at a massive discount to its book value. The bailout was an unmitigated disaster, however. ADFG lost more than 90% of its investment. Noble's stock has since been suspended and the company is the subject of an investigation.

The Hyflux and Noble sagas are parables on the hidden leverage. Investors would do well to heed the lessons.

First, the accounting treatment of hybrid instruments and fair value gains may not provide an accurate picture. Perpetual bonds are hybrid securities that do not have a maturity date. Investors hold it indefinitely until the issuer redeems it.

Singapore's accounting standards have treated perpetuals as equity and not debt. This camouflaged these liabilities and understated the debt.

Most investors in Hyflux were unaware of its debt trap. The company's financial statements indicated that it was profitable and cash flow positive until FY2017.

In FY2016, its net profit was $3.8 million. However, if one accounts for the interest due to perpetual debt holders, Hyflux had a net loss of $60 million.

Similarly, Hyflux's net gearing was just 87% in FY2016. However, if one treats the preferred equity and hybrid capital as liabilities, the net gearing was about 290%. Only the most discerning of investors were aware of the looming minefield.

As with Hyflux's view on perpetual debt, Noble's treatment of fair value gains seemed to be consistent with accounting standards. This is the practice of recording the fair value of an asset or liability based on market prices, as opposed to historical costs. The practice inflates the asset base in a bull market for commodities, providing more collateral. In FY2014, Noble's fair value gains amounted to US$5.8 billion, which was roughly equal to its equity base.

However, the commodities bear market in 2014 to 2018 led to a hole in Noble's balance sheet. Trading losses compounded the issue. Noble's credit metrics were far worse than ADFG had initially estimated.

Second, there could be similar pitfalls in Singapore's corporate bond market. Industries facing a downturn, such as commodities, property and logistics, could be exposed.

CWT is a Singapore-based logistics firm that has borne the brunt of the slowdown in global trade. It has $100 million of corporate bonds that are due in March 2020. Its Hong Kong-listed parent CWT International defaulted on a US$179 million debt in April. Creditors have seized CWT International's assets, including its stake in CWT.

Third, the success of the restructuring could hinge on the synergy benefits for the white knight. ADFG sought to buttress Noble's trading operation, but did not succeed. Hyflux's existing cash flow situation is precarious.

If Utico is successful in its bid for the company, its CEO Richard Menezes will look to slash costs. Utico has vast operations in the water sector in several Gulf countries that could complement Hyflux's core operations.

Hyflux's liabilities may fall under the deal, but its operations need to be leaner for it to succeed. A haircut alone would not do the trick; it would need a facelift to emerge from this crisis.

Postscript

Hyflux's woes continue to defy resolution. The judicial managers are still in talks with investors.

COMMODITIES

Are diamonds an investor's best friend?

Published on August 28, 2020

In the movie *Marathon Man,* an escaped Nazi tortures a student by posing as a dentist. The torturer was extracting information on stolen diamonds by pulling teeth.

The diamond industry is rife with such atrocities. Diamonds are precious and easily hidden. They are hoarded during uncertainty. The precious stones are portable and carry immense value. People routinely kill for US$100,000 ($137,152) diamond rings.

The main demand for diamonds is for courtship. Grooms feel obliged to propose with a diamond ring. The practice is ingrained in the US, which is by far the largest market for the stone. The South African company De Beers has held a tight grip on diamond production. Proposing with diamonds can be traced to a marketing campaign by De Beers in the 1930s.

The ad campaign emphasised diamond's hardness and its shine. The hardness was projected as a symbol of eternal love. The shine was linked to love's passion. The tag line "a diamond is forever" caught on.

Marathon Man was set in 1976. Diamonds then cost around US$$5,500 a carat, according to the Rapaport Diamond Index. Today, the price has doubled to US$10,229. That may sound like a hefty gain. However, adjusting for inflation, it has lost over 70% of its value since 1976. It has been an appalling investment and not a store of value.

Today's diamond market seems ripe for a rally. Diamond's status as a hedge against inflation has risen with COVID-19.

The last 44 years have seen two periods where diamond investing shone bright. Both were times of high inflation.

Between 1978 and 1980, diamonds doubled to US$65,000 in today's money. There was a similar bubble in gold and oil. After the crash of September 2008, diamonds rose 20% in the next two years. As with the boom in 1978-1980, inflation fears drove the rally. There are similarities between the COVID-19 world and the late 1970s. The fears of high inflation are high. Real interest rates are now negative. This suggests that like gold, people may flock to diamonds in the COVID-19 era.

On the demand side, China could add sparkle to the industry. China has mimicked many American rituals. Producing diamonds when proposing is one of them. Its share of the diamond market has quadrupled in the last decade to one-third. It could rise further. China has a skewed sex ratio. In some cities, there are two suitors for each eligible bride. A diamond provides a suitor with an edge. It is a signal that the groom has money.

The supply of diamonds has been weak recently. Diamonds traditionally funded wars in Sierra Leone and Angola. Children have been conscripted as soldiers. Hence, an NGO campaign sought to restrict the diamond trade.

Since 2003, 75 countries have banned the export of diamonds linked to conflict. Traders have to prove that their diamonds are conflict-free. If not, the traders could be banned. Diamond supply has fallen 15% since the blood diamond ban.

COVID-19 has worsened the supply issues. Over 90% of the world's diamonds are processed in India. The severe lockdown put 200,000 out of work. Processing has been almost decimated. A sharp shortage of diamonds seems likely. There are stock market proxies for a diamond rally. De Beers, the patron saint of diamonds, is owned by the London-listed **Anglo American PLC**.

There are signs that De Beer's tide is turning. It reported that revenue in July was 50-70% of pre-COVID-19. With lockdowns easing, it could improve further. Its parent is at half its book value.

It may be better to sell diamonds than own them. Despite the COVID-19 carnage, its Chinese retail store sales were 90% higher y-o-y in July. Tiffany has opened 34 stores in China. Operations elsewhere are returning to normal.

In our own backyard, **TLV Holdings** — a local jeweller — is trading at 0.2x P/B. TLV Holdings owns the Taka brand of jewellery. Its market capitalisation of US$20 million is a quarter of its stock of jewellery. **SK Jewellery** is another local jeweller that seems unloved at 0.3x P/B. A diamond rally may add some sparkle.

As with love, there are no guarantees in diamond investing. But, COVID-19 could finally make diamonds the investor's best friend.

Is there a silver lining to COVID-19?

Published on July 17, 2020

The ghost of Nelson Bunker Hunt has cursed the silver market for the last 40 years. Hunt, who died in 2014 at 88, was once one of the richest men in the world.

Hunt prospered in the 1960s by acquiring stud farms in Texas and oil fields in Libya. In 1969, when his holdings in Libyan oil were nationalised, Hunt turned his attention to silver.

Despite his vast trappings, Hunt had simple tastes. He drove second-hand Cadillacs and flew economy class. He was also probably the only Texas oilman who did not drink.

But his austere lifestyle hid a religious fervour. He feared an apocalypse was imminent. When that happens, money would become worthless and precious metals would surge.

In 1974, Nelson Bunker Hunt and his brother William Herbert Hunt accumulated silver. Silver was just US$1.50 an ounce (about 1% of the price of gold). In five years, the Hunt brothers had cornered 250 million ounces of silver, which was almost 50% of the world's silver.

The price had risen more than 30-fold to US$50 an ounce —an all-time high. By early 1980, the Hunts held US$4 billion worth of silver, which is worth US$12 billion ($16.7 billion) today.

The regulators took action. Congress banned margin trading in silver. The banks then made margin calls on the Hunts. On March 27, 1980, or what is now known as "Silver Thursday", a catastrophe hit the silver market. The price of silver halved to US$10.50 an ounce. The Hunts eventually declared bankruptcy in 1988.

The bitter memories of Silver Thursday have since dampened silver prices. Today, the price of silver is 90% less in real terms to its peak in 1979 and is 62% less than its price in nominal terms.

This year, the COVID-19 pandemic has driven gold prices up 19%, outperforming silver by 10%. The Gold Silver Ratio (GSR) is at 95 times, which is way above its 1980–2020 average of 65 times.

Holding gold during troubled times is a familiar mantra, but the case for silver is stronger. Gold has very few applications. It serves as an ornament and a store of wealth. Silver, by the sharpest of contrasts, is used for industrial and medical purposes as well.

The rise of digital appliances has provided a fillip to silver. About half of the world's silver is used for industrial purposes. These include electronics and solar appliances. Silver's "killer app" is that it is both light and highly conductible. It is, in fact, the most conductible of the elements. It is ideal for the emerging wearable technology market. Apple watches and activity trackers used by runners require silver. The "Internet of Things" where household items like the microwave oven can be operated through the internet, is a bonanza for silver. Solar panels also require silver.

But, the biggest demand boost for silver may be COVID-19. Silver particles are effective in killing bacteria and wiping out many infections. That is why silver nanoparticles are used in bandages and face masks.

The market may be missing a fundamental aspect of silver supply. The supply of the silver that is above ground is much smaller than that of gold. The world's gold supply consists of the entire capacity that has been mined in history. This can be found in museums, vaults or in people's wrists. The world supply of gold is about 6 billion tonnes.

On the other hand, half of the 54 billion ounces silver mined has been consumed or destroyed. Only about a tenth of the remaining 24 billion tonnes is investible. The rest is in jewellery, silverware and statues.

This makes silver far scarcer than its better-known cousin. Indeed, silver prices rose five-fold in the three years from May 2008 with the 2008 Global Financial Cisis driving up silver prices.

There are ETFs that track the silver price. SLV ETF that trades on NYSE is the most popular.

Investing in stocks that produce silver may provide even better returns than chasing the commodity. During the 2008–2011 silver boom, silver producers Great Panther Mining (NYSE: GPL) and First Majestic Silver (NYSE: AG) rose about 30-fold.

Silver now has applications that were unheard of in Hunt's era. It is time to bury the 1980 silver crash. Hunt may finally be proven right. A calamity like a pandemic may cause a silver boom.

Postscript

My silver pitch has yet to work out. However, it is early days. The post-pandemic inflation trade may play out in 2021. It is too early to dismiss this precious metal.

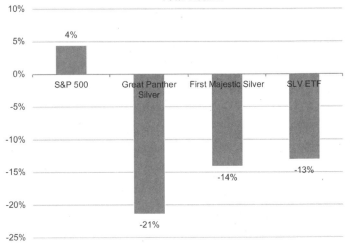

Total Return

S&P 500	4%
Great Panther Silver	-21%
First Majestic Silver	-14%
SLV ETF	-13%

Lithium may rise like a meteor

Published on September 11, 2020

Chadwick Boseman, the star of the *Black Panther* movie, died a fortnight ago on Aug 28. He succumbed to cancer at just 43. His fans may be comforted by the real life equivalent of the commodity featured in the movie.

Black Panther is set in a fictional African country called Wakanda. Boseman plays T'Challa, the charismatic heir to the throne.

Wakanda is a rich country. It resembles the Dubai skyline surrounded by the greenery of *The Jungle Book*.

The source of Wakanda's wealth is a fictional metal called Vibranium, which has a magical quality that make it indestructible. The metal can absorb lethal forces. Bullets bounce off T'Chala's Vibranium armour. Vibranium rods split mountains in half.

There is no such metal in reality. However, Vibranium may be a metaphor for a commodity that may have arrived.

Tesla Inc, the pioneer in electric vehicles, may lead us to the Vibranium of today—lithium. Even though there was a sharp correction earlier this week, Tesla has seen its stock price triple since the middle of March. Like Vibranium, Tesla has its origins in Africa. Its founder Elon Musk is a South African who made his Wakanda-esque fortune in the US.

As at September 9, Tesla has a market capitalisation of US$307 billion ($420.8 billion). This exceeds the market cap of the next four largest automakers. Tesla's staggering rise reflects the seismic transformation in the auto world. Tesla's 2QFY2020 sales were solid in the middle of a pandemic. In contrast, traditional autos like **General Motors Company** have floundered.

Citibank expects Tesla's sales to rise at a CAGR of 19% in the next five years. This is four times the projected growth for traditional autos. EV sales are rising across the board including Bayerische Motoren Werke and Toyota Motor Corp.

EVs will be powered by lithium. Lithium has indestructible features because of the economics of electric vehicles. Electric cars are cheap to operate. It costs only two cents a mile to operate. Petrol powered cars are six times as expensive to run.

However, the batteries have been pricey. A single charge can sustain a car for 250 miles. That is about six gallons of petrol.

Technology is moving rapidly in favour of lithium batteries. Tesla's lithium ion batteries cost about US$1,200 per kilowatt hour. Tesla is about to launch a so-called Million Mile Battery, which would cut the battery cost to US$100 per kilowatt hour. Lithium would then emerge as the powerhouse of the auto industry.

Tesla's ascent this year has not been matched by a rise in lithium prices. Due to active expansion in production, lithium prices are down almost 70% from the 2017 peak of US$20,000 a tonne to US$6,500 a tonne.

The gut-wrenching collapse should not deter us. The case for lithium is rock solid in the pandemic. COVID-19 may lead to a recession, but climate change will still be an issue. EVs are not just cheaper, but they are less pollutive.

A vast array of incentives will support EVs. Governments will punish traditional vehicles with high charges. In Europe, EVs are already exempt from taxes. In the US, EV owners are eligible for up to US$7,500 in state tax breaks.

Lithium has a narrow supply base, compared to oil. Supply growth has been relatively low in the last decade. Oil and gas have dominated commodity investment.

Tesla can produce up to 1.5 million EVs per year till 2025. Others will produce a similar amount. If so, the demand for lithium would double its supply by 2025.

Direct investment in lithium is a challenge. Unlike oil and gas, you cannot buy lithium in a commodity exchange. Futures contracts and swaps are rare.

The best way to play lithium may be through listed companies. The largest lithium producer is a Chilean company listed on the NYSE—**Sociedad Quimica y Minera de Chile** (SQM). It also produces chemicals, which dilutes the lithium exposure.

There is an ETF that tracks lithium stocks—**Global X Lithium**. The ETF is up 35% this year, but that is partly because it includes Tesla. Its major holdings include SQM and American lithium producers **FMC Corp** and **Albemarle Corp**.

Wakanda's prosperity has its origins in a meteor that landed with Vibranium. Tesla's ascent may be that meteor for lithium.

Postscript

Lithium has risen sharply. It is a commodity with a new economy momentum behind it. Investors view it as a proxy for the EV revolution.

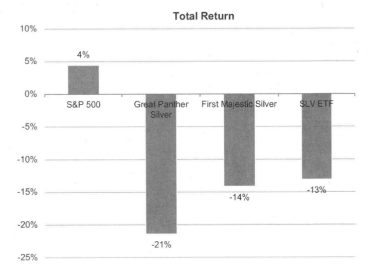

Total Return

S&P 500: 4%
Great Panther Silver: -21%
First Majestic Silver: -14%
SLV ETF: -13%

Rubber could bounce from the glove boom

Published on July 30, 2020

"During the gold rush, it is a good time to be in the pick and shovel business." — Mark Twain

As the shares of glove makers skyrocket, a rubber rally seems imminent. Investors would be well-served to heed the lessons of an old British soldier.

Algy Cluff made his money in North Sea oil and African gold. At 80, there is still much petrol left in his tank. He has just launched a new African oil venture after a glittering run as the Chairman of London-listed Cluff Gold.

Cluff is tall, lean and always polite. His wife joked that he should change his name to Club, as he spent so much time on them. Despite his stately manner, luck played its part in Cluff's ascent.

He owes his success to a chance meeting in the Long Bar of the Raffles Hotel in 1961. Cluff, then 21, was a Major in the British Army. While he was sampling the Singapore Sling, he ran into Charles Letts, a 46-year-old Scotsman.

Letts was a trader who was established in the Straits Settlements. He was fluent in Malayan commerce, as well as Hokkien, Thai and Malay. Letts persuaded the young Cluff to invest in rubber companies. The Malayan rubber companies were trading at well below their book values. Rubber prices were likely to rise with the explosion in tyre demand.

The conversation prompted Cluff to get his father Harold to invest in Malayan rubber stocks. The rubber stocks rose sharply, as the demand for tyres rose. The value of the land held by the rubber plantations appreciated. The rubber price increased threefold in the 1960s, but the rubber stock prices rose sixfold.

When Cluff left the army, his father let him keep the profits. It meant that the young man did not need to take a job. He could focus on business. The rubber profits seeded Cluff's foray into oil, gas and gold.

Today, rubber is similarly placed to its level in 1961. Instead of rubber tyres, the swing factor is now from rubber gloves. COVID-19 has led to a scramble for rubber gloves. **Top Glove Corp**, the largest rubber glove producer in the world, has seen a surge in orders. It was previously running at less than 70% capacity. Today, its 44 factories are operating 24 hours a day, seven days a week. It is servicing orders from as many as 195 countries. Top Glove has surged 445% this year. It is now the second largest company on the KLSE. Another glove producer Malaysian rubber producer **SuperMax** is up over 1000%.

There are two types of rubber—natural rubber and synthetic rubber. Each type has production of about 13 million tonnes. The prices of the two categories move in tandem, as synthetic rubber requires natural rubber. Natural rubber is the main ingredient for most types of tyres. About 70% of natural rubber is met by tyres. The remaining 30% is made up of gloves, condoms and other sanitary applications.

Natural rubber prices are 80% below its 2010 high of US$6,100 ($8,403). At a price of US$1,300 per ton, rubber is still only marginally above its cost of production. Prices have been weak for the last six years. The rubber route since 2014 is due to misplaced fears of a Chinese slowdown. The craving for cars in China is unlikely to end with COVID-19. Only a third of China's families own a car. This is less than half the level in the US in 1920. If the car population doubles in China by 2030, rubber production will have to rise by 50%. Natural rubber demand fell 20% in 1H2020 due to COVID-19. But China, which represents 40% of rubber demand, is showing signs of recovery.

Investors may seek exposure to rubber through the listed proxies. **Halcyon Agri**, the world's largest rubber processor, is listed on the SGX. It is controlled by Sinochem, a Chinese state-owned enterprise that has rubber plantations in West Africa. Halcyon Agri operating performance is exposed to the natural rubber prices.

Other processors include **Sri Trang Agro** listed in Thailand and Singapore. Sri Trang has just completed a US$480 million IPO of its glove unit. The rubber price may be about to bounce even harder. Discerning investors could replicate Cluff's success without going to the Long Bar.

Postscript
Rubber prices have fallen, but Halcyon Agri has rallied. The case for rubber remains intact. It could recover with the post-pandemic recovery.

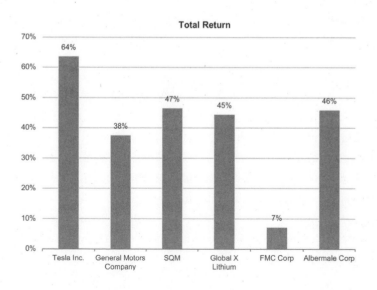

Altman casts dark shadow over Singapore's oil and gas sector

Published on June 19, 2020

In the summer of 2015, I met Professor Ed Altman at a lecture in New York. He had founded the Altman Z-score in 1968, a popular formula for predicting bankruptcy.

Altman's gentle manner belied a titanic drive. As a PhD student in 1965, he was struggling to find a thesis topic. His professor sent him a single word note with "bankruptcy" written on it. Academic studies on the causes of bankruptcy were then rare. Altman was inspired to create an index that would rate the default probability of corporations.

Raw data was hard to get in the pre-Internet era. He had to patiently read through thousands of pages of annual reports. This was long before Bloomberg and Edgar. Pen, paper and the slide rule were the main tools (not Excel). Altman was determined to collate the data.

Altman first published his Z-score formula 52 years ago. It is a combination of profitability, leverage, liquidity, solvency, and activity ratios. Its founder did not expect the metric to become the gold standard for bankruptcy analysis.

It has proved to be an excellent predictor of bankruptcy. Many high-profile bankruptcies have been identified by the metric, including Enron and WorldCom. The Altman Z-score marked out Hertz as a distressed company months before it filed for bankruptcy last month.

Though Altman's Z-score was initially directed at American companies, it provides clues for Singapore's volatile oil and gas sector.

Singapore has become the world's largest maker of jack-up rigs. These are used to drill for oil in shallow ocean waters.

Singapore's oil and gas sector has been on shaky ground since the oil collapse of 2014. The COVID-19 pandemic has worsened the situation.

The bear market for oil since 2014 has led rig builders to slash jobs and capacity. Some of the 42 listed oil and gas players have already gone belly up. Swiber Holdings, a prominent marine engineering company, was placed under a court-supervised rescue plan in 2016. Swiber defaulted on coupon payment. A restructured Swiber is still struggling with an Altman Z-score deep in the danger zone. Ezra Holdings filed for bankruptcy in the following year.

COVID-19 has magnified the leverage issues of these companies. It has contracted their ability to service debt and worsened the working capital situation.

The recent oil rally has been kind to the oil and gas sector. It has risen 14% from its lows in March. But, we are not out of the woods.

The Altman Z-score has three zones. A Z-score of above 2.99 is the safe zone. Between 2.99 and 1.81 is the grey zone. Below 1.8 is the danger zone. The Singapore oil and gas sector holds an average Z-score of 0.2, which is deep within the distress range. Admittedly, the Altman Z-score is backward looking. It does not capture the improved cash flow from a prospective oil rally.

The Altman Z-score seemed to be a prescient predictor of the distress in the oil and gas sector. Swiber's descent into receivership was preceded by its fall into the Altman danger zone.

A vibrant oil recovery could improve the cash flow of the sector. Also, there have been severe cuts in capacity. That could be the seed of improved operating earnings.

However, investors may stay clear of the companies with the vulnerabilities that the Z-score reveals. The sector includes rig builders and marine engineers. **Sembcorp Marine**, **Triyards** and **KS Energy** are in the distress zone.

These firms have a high proportion of net working capital to assets. This lends itself to a dependence on short-term debt. Sembcorp Marine has a total debt of US$4.7 billion ($6.5 billion) and its Ebitda was barely sufficient to meet its interest payments in FY19.

It may be enticing to dabble in a sector that is at a 60% discount to its peak. But, the debt ratios of many Singapore oil and gas companies are alarming.

As the labour of a 79-year-old professor indicates, Singaporean investors should tread with caution.

Postscript

Sembcorp Marine has fallen due to its debt. Singapore's oil and gas space remains in the doldrums.

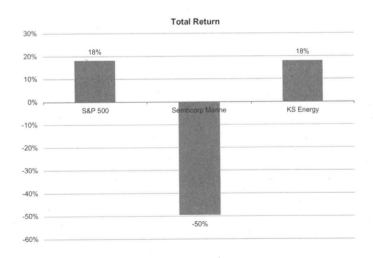

Why did Hin Leong collapse?

Published on April 24, 2020

Nick Leeson, the trader who blew up Barings Bank in 1995, was fond of Harry's Bar in Boat Quay. He used to sample the cocktails to take the sting out of the day.

He had a constant worry in those steamy evenings at the bar. Leeson needed to cover his tracks. The US$1 billion of losses that he hid in February 1995 were not the first time that he had engaged in these practices.

It was just that a vile series of events — including the Kobe earthquake that tanked the Japanese market — that made it impossible to hide his misdeeds.

Hin Leong Trading, an oil trader owned by Singaporean billionaire OK Lim, is facing bankruptcy with debts of US$4 billion ($5.71 billion). The private company is seeking protection from creditors. If this is granted, Hin Leong will have two weeks to work out a restructuring programme with the banks.

Like Nick Leeson, OK Lim has been hiding US$800 million losses for years, according to his affidavit. He had instructed his finance department to camouflage the trading losses by placing it in the receivables. It was done so well that it took an unprecedented commodity collapse to bring the misdeeds to light.

Hin Leong — which means 'prosperity' in Chinese — is a titan in the bunker fuel field. It has risen in tandem with Singapore's emergence as one of the world's busiest ports. It was founded in 1963 by Lim, who first began supplying ships with marine fuel by driving his own truck.

Bunker fuel prices have fallen 65% YTD, as many ships are stagnant with trade coming to a halt. Hin Leong was not hedged against the rout.

Commodity traders play a similar role to **DHL** and **FedEx**. They are the delivery boys of the commodity world. During the decade-long commodity bull run that began in 2004, traders were coveted by investors as Singapore is a major centre for commodity traders. There are tax incentives for traders that establish their global headquarters in the city-state.

Several commodity traders such as **Wilmar International**, **Olam International** and **Noble Group** are listed on the SGX. These traders carry inventory, which may be exposed to the commodity collapse.

The earnings of commodity traders were said to be protected from commodity swings as earnings growth would be driven by a volume expansion. Investors thus coveted commodity traders such as Wilmar, **Glencore** and Noble.

However, the enthusiasm was misplaced and this error is now being exposed by the commodity rout.

Actually, the profits of commodity traders are intensely correlated with the commodity price. Between 2004 to 2014, the S&P Goldman Sachs Commodity Index (S&P GSCI) rose two and a half times. The operating profits of the major commodity traders such as Noble, Glencore and Olam increased on a similar scale. Since 2014, operating profits have fallen by an average of 34% in the peer group, as the S&P GSCI has dropped 59% in the past six years.

Commodity traders profit from the spread between a seller and buyer of a commodity. The spread may be steady in proportionate terms. However, it will vary in absolute terms with the swings in commodity prices.

The risks in the business can be contained if the trader restricts itself to the role of middleman. However, vulnerabilities arise when a commodity trader speculates with its inventory.

The difficulty arises when a commodity trader speculates on commodity prices—it is dangerous because the prices can be violently volatile, as Hin Leong's travails show.

The dirty secret of the bunker fuel traders were on display to Singaporean investors when Chemoil Energy, a bunker fuel trader, listed on SGX in 2007. It was founded by Bob Chandran, a businessman from India who had the swagger and drive of a Texan oilman.

Chandran had the wisdom to transform Chemoil Energy from a trader to an operator of bunkering facilities in Los Angeles, Fujairah and Singapore. But, Chemoil Energy also carried about two weeks of inventory on its books. Still, it actively traded this inventory. Within two quarters of its listing, trading losses shook the business.

Investing in some commodity traders has similar risks to investing in a gambler. They outperform in bull markets but can unravel in a collapse. It is no wonder that Leeson sought solace in Harry's cocktails, while he fretted about the losses that he had hid.

Postscript

Commodity traders have risks that have been exposed in the pandemic. These players have performed poorly.

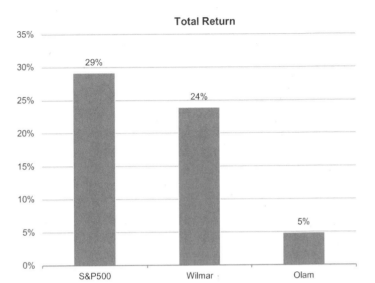

Total Return

How to play nickel's turnaround

Published on September 13, 2016

Nickel is the only commodity that is named after the devil. The name Nickel is derived from the German term "*Kupfernickel*", which means devil's copper. From the 15th century, miners mistook nickel for copper ore. Miners were fooled by the red colour. The disappointed miners blamed Old Nick—a pseudonym for the devil.

Swedish chemist Axel Cronstedt identified nickel as an element in 1751. He tried to extract copper but found a white metal instead. This white metal is what we now call nickel.

Nickel has been at the heart of industrialisation and is the principal component for steel production. The discovery of stainless steel in the early 20th century provided nickel with a killer app. The vast storage tanks that transport oil are made of stainless steel. Modern skyscrapers would not exist without it.

Also, alloys based on nickel are resistant to corrosion. Its non-corrosive quality made it eminently suited for chemical plants and jet engines. Nickel has been devilishly volatile and one of the worst-hit commodities as the resource bull run evaporated. It suffered from weakening demand and excess supply.

Nickel prices collapsed 40% in 2015. More than half of nickel producers are losing money at the current price of US$10,231 a tonne. Last year's US$5 billion ($6.7 billion) net loss at giant commodity trader Glencore was due mainly to a write-down at a nickel project.

The fall in stainless steel demand in China, the main market, is the dark cloud over nickel. About a third of China's steel capacity is unsustainable, with the halt in real estate demand. Chinese stainless steel demand has fallen 9% in the year ended June 2016.

But China's travails are only part of the demand. ASEAN, a region that has been relegated to irrelevance during the commodity super cycle, may be nickel's salvation.

Indonesia, Thailand, Malaysia, the Philippines and Vietnam have a combined GDP of US$2.3 trillion and could rise a third by 2020 to US$3 trillion.

GDP growth of this magnitude will drive infrastructure development. There is dire need for airports, dams and railways in the emerging markets of this region. Steel demand is a direct beneficiary of the infrastructure buildout.

Thailand's military government is planning US$50 billion in infrastructure spending. Vietnam has just embarked on a US$10 billion rail upgrade. Indonesia is building out the largest road expansion in its history. New Filipino President Rodrigo Duterte has vowed to double rail and airport capacity during his term.

The new demand from the ASEAN region would absorb the excess Chinese steel supply. Already, China's steel exports have reached unprecedented levels in 2016. India may also import more nickel, along with the surge in ASEAN, where steel demand may grow at 6% in 2016 and 2017. At 75 million tonnes, project demand from the region will exceed that of Africa and the Middle East. **Fortescue Metals Group** recently reiterated that China had no monopoly on steel demand growth. Emerging ASEAN and India could step into the breach.

There is also an imminent supply constraint in the region that could boost nickel. In 2014, Indonesia banned raw mineral ore exports to promote the local processing industry. The ban cut global exports by a tenth.

A similar move seems likely in the Philippines. Duterte has a deep desire to wipe out crime using severe means and has modelled himself on Dirty Harry, the vigilante played by Clint Eastwood. This ruthless drive to eliminate criminals seems to have extended to the mining industry.

Duterte has appointed extreme environmentalist Gina Lopez as Environment and Natural Resources Secretary. Lopez is intent on closing down mines that fail to satisfy her standards. Eight nickel ore mines have been closed. A nationwide audit due this month threatens further closures. The closures in the Philippines amount to about 2% of world supply. It could tip the nickel industry into shortage. A fillip to nickel prices may be around the corner.

There is a nickel exchange-traded fund that replicates the direction of the commodity. Investors may want to turn, however, to listed nickel proxies in the region. **Global Ferronickel Holdings**, the second-largest nickel producer in the Philippines, is down 76% since its peak in December. It has vastly underperformed the market. It has high operating standards and an aggressive management.

The miners in the 1500s saw the devil's hand when they mistook nickel for copper. By writing off nickel because of China's slowdown, investors may be making a similar mistake. It is time to dodge the devil.

Postscript

Nickel prices have defied the commodity gloom. Nickel's rally is due to ore shortages and massive demand from China's steel mills.

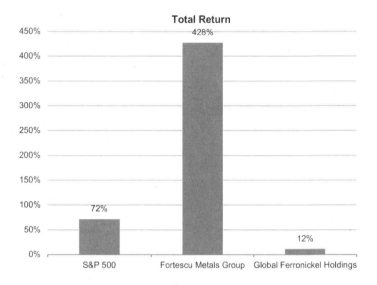

What Brexit teaches about commodity investing

Published on June 28, 2016

Mike Tyson said "everybody has a plan until they get punched in the face". He could have been describing the strife in the commodity markets after Brexit. Brexit has led to a 15% spike in the US dollar versus the Pound. As many of the world's commodities are denominated in US dollars, a strong dollar is negative for commodities. On the flip side, gold has risen by 12% to its highest point in five years. The commodities that trade in pounds such as cocoa and natural gas have risen sharply.

Brexit reminds us that commodity investing is as much a play on currencies as it is on demand and supply. Commodity prices are a function of the currency that they trade.

The Plaza Accord of September 1985 was reminiscent of the Brexit shock. It exposed the vulnerability of commodities to currency shocks. Though it was barely 30 years ago, the world was radically different. China and the Soviet Union were isolated from Japan and the West. The term emerging markets was an obscure euphemism for Third World countries. The rise of the Asian giants China and India was a generation away.

The backdrop to the Accord was a five-year surge in the value of the US dollar. The greenback had skyrocketed by 50% against the Yen from 1980 to 1985. American industry were facing hard times, as they were uncompetitive. The US current account deficit had swelled to 3.5% of GDP. The US was in the throes of a crippling recession, which belied the sunny optimism of then President Ronald Reagan.

A broad coalition of grain exporters, tech companies and auto manufacturers lobbied for a devaluation. This included industry leaders such as Ford, IBM and Cargill. The pressure on the Republican administration culminated in the Plaza Accord.

It was an agreement between France, West Germany, Japan, USA and UK that was signed at the Plaza Hotel in New York City. The governments agreed to depreciate the US dollar versus the Yen and Deutsche Mark. This was the first time that the world's five leading economies had agreed to intervene in the currency markets. It was also the first occasion that these economies set target exchange rates.

In the next two years the Dollar lost 51% of its value against the Yen. The collapse in the Dollar's value made American tourists in Japan feel like Third World visitors to the West. A dizzying property bubble culminated in a gravity-defying boom in Japan.

As most commodities are denominated in US dollars, commodity prices spiked sharply. Oil price rose 25% in the three months after the Plaza accord. The impact on the Bloomberg Commodity Index was even stronger, at 33%.

But, the currency-driven spike was brief. By early 1986, the demand-supply dynamics that drive commodities regained ascendancy. The Saudis were intent on a price war with the US. They raised production and drove oil prices down by 67%. Oil fell from US$25 a barrel to US$10 a barrel in a few months. Saudi regained its position as the largest oil producer. The American industry was in tatters, triggering 25 years of declining production.

The Brexit fallout is hauntingly similar to that of the Plaza Accord, but in reverse. Brexit has been positive for the dollar. The Dollar-denominated commodities have fallen in Brexit's wake. Gold and a handful of commodities such as natural gas and cocoa that are denominated in Sterling have appreciated.

But the fundamental case for a new commodity cycle cannot be dislodged by currency moves. Just as the Plaza accord had a short-lived impact on commodities, Brexit may prove to be a fleeting event.

Speculators are betting that oil will fall to US$45 a barrel from its pre-Brexit high of US$50 a barrel. The Bloomberg consensus is that copper will fall another 20% in the next fortnight.

These fears are unfounded. Commodity producers from Shell to Rio Tinto are cutting their capital expenditure to meet their dividend obligations. Shale drillers are retreating from production in the US.

Brexit will have a negligible impact on oil consumption. Britain consumes just 2% of the world's oil. Europe represents 14% of total oil consumption. The chance of Brexit causing a worldwide slump in oil consumption is slim. The global demand for commodities is not contingent on the intricacies of a free trade agreement. Commodity investors may have received a nasty blow to their jaws, but that should not deter them from boxing on.

Postscript

Commodity prices have been steady after the Brexit vote. They have risen but have underperformed the stock market.

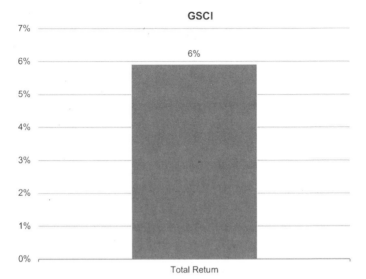

El Niño may create a rice price spike

Published on December 1, 2015

The year 1997 is remembered for the death of Princess Diana. That was not the only catastrophe in that year. There was El Niño, which wreaked considerable havoc.

Eighteen years later, a severe El Niño is looming. El Niño is a climatic condition that occurs in the Pacific region. The basic outcome of El Niño is exceptionally dry weather. El Niño occurs when weakening trade winds allow the warmer water from the western Pacific Ocean to flow east. Seas become shallower. It causes a build-up of warm surface water off the coast of South America. This increases the water temperature in Southeast Asia.

The higher water temperature alters the weather of this region. The clouds associated with warm ocean waters also shift eastward. Thus, rains that normally would fall over Indonesia, occurs in Peru. This causes drought in Southeast Asia, while South America faces floods.

In 1997, there was intense drought and flooding. One-sixth of the world's reef systems were destroyed. Air temperature rose by 1.5 degrees Centigrade, which is six times the normal impact of an El Niño episode. Southeast Asia was at the epicentre of the crisis. Indonesia faced the hottest year in its recorded history. A crippling drought paralysed agriculture. That might have hastened Suharto's fall.

Now, meteorologists fear that this El Niño will match 1997 in its severity. Last week, El Niño claimed its first victim—China Fishery Group. China Fishery Group is a Singapore-listed fishing company with operations in coastal Peru. HSBC, one of China Fishery's creditors, initiated bankruptcy proceedings last Thursday. Two weeks ago, Moody's downgraded China Fishery's debt due to El Niño concerns.

El Niño can devastate fishing in South America's Pacific Coast. According to Undercurrentnews.com, an industry website, China Fishery was completely exposed to it, as over 60% of its fishing is in Northern Peru. China Fishery lacked the cash to cover operating costs and debt obligations, including US$300 million in short-term debt that was due in 2016.

China Fishery's travails might be an omen. El Niño could affect a commodity at the heart of Asian consumption – rice. In Asia, a region that consumes four-fifths of the world's rice, the repercussions could be enormous.

While rice is widely consumed, it is narrowly traded internationally. Only 7% of the world's rice traded across borders. Thailand is the largest rice exporter with about a third of the market. As it is driven by government diktat rather than market forces, rice supply is volatile. Government intervention in Thailand in 2008 pushed prices as high as US$1,038 per tonne, which is three times today's price.

This year's El Niño could reduce rice exports. In Thailand, the drought could cripple production growth. Thai rice exports were down 25% ytd, according to USDA. Futures markets are already indicating a rice surge. US rice futures on the Chicago Board of Trade are up 23% in the last six months. The futures market has yet to sway the spot market. Export prices for Thai rice are up only 4% ytd.

There are hardly any listed rice companies in the region. Instead, wheat-based noodle companies may provide a proxy. Indonesia's wheat consumption growth has outstripped rice consumption growth since 2005. The average Indonesian eats about 76kg per annum. Wheat consumption is barely over 20kg per capita but could rise sharply.

Indofood Consumer Branded Products (ICBP) pioneered noodles in Indonesia by branding traditional flavours such as Nasi Goreng. It has a vice-like grip on the market.

It is now still cheaper to eat a bowl of rice than a packet of instant noodles. But a rice price spike could be a boon for the noodle companies. The rice crisis in 2007-2008 saw rice prices quadruple in four months. In 2008, the rice-wheat price differential widened to USD 700/t. If that recurs, ICPB could see a sudden spurt in demand.

2016 may be remembered for its noodle boom.

Postscript

The case for noodle stocks has worked out. It is a cheap and convenient product. ICBP has solid cash flows.

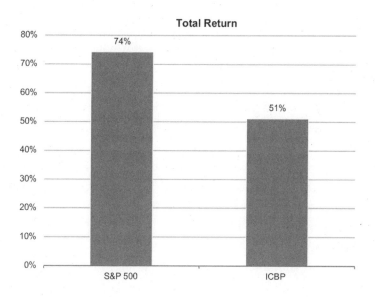

Palm Oil Slavery

Published on October 21, 2015

The thick haze over Singapore has sparked a backlash against Indonesian companies. Last month, the National Environmental Agency (NEA) accused at least six Indonesian companies of starting forest fires. Last week, Singaporean retailers NTUC, Prime and Sheng Shiong removed products linked to one of the suspected companies from their shelves. Meanwhile, Indonesian authorities have taken action against a number of companies, including some palm oil producers.

Interestingly, the palm oil trade traces its roots back to a similar campaign in Britain more than 200 years ago against the slave trade. In the 1700s, Liverpool was at the centre of a vast slave enterprise, known as the triangular trade. Slaves were captured from West Africa and sent across the Atlantic to work in the West Indian plantations. Sugar, tobacco and cotton were produced by slave labour. These commodities were then exported to Britain and to the rest of the empire.

West Indian islands such as Jamaica and Trinidad rapidly became massive labour camps. In Jamaica, the number of sugar plantations rose from 70 plantations in 1672 to 680 plantations in 1770. In 1800, there were 21,000 Englishmen ruling over 300,000 African slaves on the island.

British consumers had a boundless appetite for the slave products, particularly sugar. Like caviar today, sugar was once a delicacy in Europe. However, in the 18th century, production boomed due to slave labour and it became a consumer product. Cake, chocolate and tarts became widely available.

William Wilberforce, an ambitious and virtuous British MP, was repulsed by the inhumanity of slavery. He meticulously documented the cruelty of the enterprise and campaigned against it. Yet, much like those who defend slash-and-burn clearing in Indonesia as a legitimate practice, slavery had powerful patrons in the 1790s. Pro-slavery advocates in Britain claimed that the victims were lesser beings and that slavery was their salvation.

Wilberforce's attempts to ban the slave trade in Parliament failed in 1792. Undeterred, he began appealing to consumers in England to boycott sugar. In the 1790s, some 300,000 people boycotted sugar and some shops only stocked Indian sugar, which was not produced by slaves.

The movement soon began to achieve its aims. Sugar planters that relied on slave labour began to lose money. In March 1807, the slave trade was banned in the British Empire.

African slaves were not the only beneficiaries of the ban. Palm oil, a product that was native to West Africa, had been neglected during the slave era. With the end of the lucrative slave trade, the Liverpool slave traders shifted their attention to West African palm oil. Palm oil was a vital ingredient for soap, a product that was gaining in demand. The railways of the British Empire also required palm oil as a lubricant. Other uses of palm oil included cooking oil, which now forms the mainstay of palm oil application.

By the early 1900s, the fulcrum of palm oil trade started to shift from West Africa to Southeast Asia. Though the plant was indigenous to Africa, the supply of labour had been decimated by the slave trade. The British preferred palm oil to continue as a wild crop in West Africa.

British Malaya, where rubber plantations were firmly entrenched, became the centre of palm oil. Today, this region produces four-fifths of the world's palm oil. Now, just as the

British craving for sugar drove the slave trade, the forest fires are rooted in the demand for fried food. Palm oil is the cheapest source of cooking oil. Soybean oil, a close substitute, typically trades at a US$100-300/t premium to palm oil.

So, will the consumer boycotts against palm oil producers drive them out of business the way Wilberforce's efforts ended the slave trade? Do not bet on it.

Ironically, the haze is hurting productivity in the palm oil sector. Palm-based biodiesel has just received a fillip too and is soaking up supply. Indonesia will impose an export levy of US$50/t for CPO and US$30/t for refined products. About two-thirds of Indonesia's 33 million tonnes are currently exported. The levy would be used to support biodiesel producers and usage of biodiesel in Indonesia could double in two years. The ratio of inventory to usage could collapse to the lowest level in a decade. Palm oil prices could jump to US$750/t next year from US$630/t today.

Nevertheless, faced with angry consumers, major palm oil producers are vowing to combat forest fires. Investors should look beyond the haze and embrace an industry that rose from the embers of slavery.

Postscript

Palm oil has rallied, despite poor commodity prices. It is the cheapest source of vegetable oil. Asia's hungry consumers are a reliable source of demand.

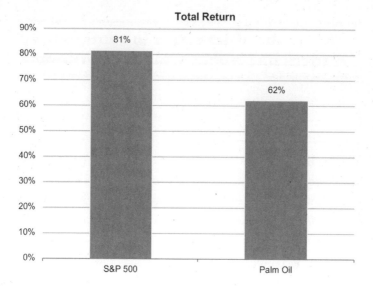

Total Return

S&P 500	81%
Palm Oil	62%

The myths of investing in commodity traders like Noble, Olam and Wilmar

Published on June 1, 2015

Warren Buffett once said, "It is only when the tide goes out that you discover who's been swimming naked." With the collapse of commodity prices in the past couple of years, it seems that commodity traders have been caught with their pants down.

At their core, commodity traders such as Singapore-listed Wilmar International, Olam International and Noble Group as well as London-listed Glencore plc are the middlemen of the commodity sector. Like DHL and FedEx, they deliver everything from oil and iron ore to corn and wheat all over the world. Glencore, for instance, supplies half the world's copper. In 2013, the 10 largest commodity trading firms generated more than US$1.3 trillion in revenue.

Once privately held businesses, a string of commodity traders went public during the decade-long commodity boom that began in 2004. And, as they came to market, they were feted by financiers. Their allure was that their earnings were supposedly immune to commodity price swings. All they had to do was increase the scale of their operations and earnings growth would follow. With pumped-up market valuations, these companies acquired upstream assets to become more integrated commodity players.

Wilmar, a soybean-focused commodity trader, went public at 80 cents. The stock skyrocketed to $7.00 in 2010. At one point, the company operating out of a Spartan office in Singapore's Chinatown had a market capitalisation greater that Kenya's GDP.

Now, the collapse in commodity prices has not only sparked a big sell-off in commodity traders, but also raised questions about their accounting practices. In recent weeks, Noble has been under fire from a shadowy research outfit called Iceberg Research. Muddy Waters, a short-seller, has joined the fray. In essence, Iceberg Research is alleging that Noble has been materially understating its debt and exaggerating its asset values. The most serious accusation is that Noble used mark-to-market accounting to record profits from long-term contracts.

Noble has denied these allegations and has taken legal action. In my view, many investors have founded their judgement of commodity traders on little more than myth. Here are some that ought to be dispelled:

Myth #1: They are neutral to commodity prices.

Reality: Companies like Noble, Glencore and Olam make money from the spread between a seller and buyer of a commodity. The spread may be constant in proportionate terms but fluctuates wildly with the swings in commodity prices.

Myth #2: They are stable and transparent because commodity prices are freely available.

Reality: Commodity traders are buccaneering enterprises that have sometimes profited in controversial ways. For instance, Marc Rich & Co., the forerunner of Glencore, first established its reputation by supplying commodities to pariah regimes such as Israel and South Africa in the 1970s. The founder Marc Rich died in exile in Switzerland after spending most of his last years as a fugitive from American justice. Other commodity traders such as Olam and Wilmar were privately held family enterprises. It was only during the commodity boom that they went public.

Myth #3: They are "operators" not speculators.

Reality: Trading in commodities is not particularly risky as long as the trader nets off its trades with buyers. If so, the trader can generate a predictable stream of earnings. Yet, speculation is the lifeblood of commodity traders, and many traders clearly do boost their margins by taking some risk. For instance, Wilmar's pre-tax earnings from refining bear little resemblance to the refining margins of the industry.

What does all this mean for investors? Are commodity traders too risky? Should they be listed at all?

In my view, investing in these companies is akin to betting on a gambler. With every successful quarter, the risk of a black swan event persists. Shares in commodity traders will outperform during commodity bull markets but can quickly fall during a commodity rout. Crucially, investors ought to distinguish between earnings these companies derive from the operating sides of their business and the gains they generate from trading.

Of course, there is little interest in reality when the market is booming. I know this only too well having covered commodity traders as an equity analyst from 2005 to 2010 at ABN Amro (later known as RBS). In 2008, I questioned Olam's high net gearing, heavy receivable burden and exposure to illiquid commodities such as cashews. In 2010, I also pointed out that over 43% of Olam's net profit was driven by concessions received from African governments.

My concerns were dismissed by the company and its shareholders. Vindication came years later though. In November 2012, Muddy Waters issued a report that alleged accounting irregularities at Olam. The company subsequently reduced its gearing and improved its disclosure, and its major shareholder Temasek Holdings hiked its stake.

The stock recovered after the controversy but is still 41% below its 2010 peak.

To paraphrase Buffett, the tide has clearly gone out on the commodity traders, and the naked truth is now there for everyone to see.

Postscript

Commodity traders have suffered in the commodity rout. Their risks have been magnified. Noble, one of the companies mentioned in this piece, lost more than 94%. It has been suspended from trading on the SGX and is subject to an investigation. Wilmar has rallied but underperformed.

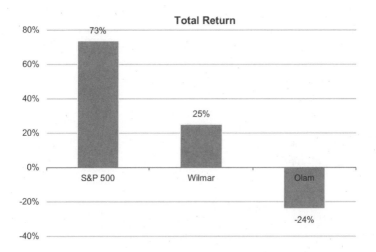

Exxon Mobil's lesson on riding the cycle

Published on June 6, 2016

The commodity super cycle has come to a brutal end. The Bloomberg commodity index is now 64% below its peak. Oil companies are floundering. Mining companies are idle and debt-laden. But it is darkest before dawn. With the end of the commodity super cycle, a new commodity cycle is emerging.

The dramatic bounce back in commodity prices from the lows of February shows the dangers of writing off this asset class. Fossil fuels remain the main source of energy. There is no viable alternative despite the fond hopes of environmentalists.

In fact, oil has nearly doubled in price since the lows of January. In the week of May 30, oil crossed US$50 a barrel. The oil glut seems to be ending.

There is value in commodities and in the venerable oil majors. ExxonMobil, one of the largest oil majors, underlines the durability of these companies. Its success is not a function of a single cycle. Instead, it has outperformed the Standard & Poor's 500 by 38% in the last 30 years.

In the last 20 years, it has returned US$180 billion (in inflation-adjusted terms) in dividends to its shareholders. This is more than the market capitalisation of all but 20 of the US corporations. Ironically, Exxon is an oil giant that emerged from the dismantling of a behemoth. In 1911, the US Supreme Court broke up Standard Oil as it unjustly dominated the oil business. Standard Oil had controlled 90% of the US oil market. Its founder, John D. Rockefeller, was tight-fisted and immensely ambitious.

Standard Oil was broken up into 34 companies. The largest of the "baby Standards" was Standard Oil of New Jersey. This company marketed products that were branded as Esso, Enco and Exxon. Exxon became the principal brand after 1973 and, eventually, the company's name.

In 1999, Exxon merged with its smaller competitor Mobil Oil in a deal worth US$73 billion. The combined entity had more energy reserves than Canada. The cost savings alone amounted to US$1.2 billion. The oil industry had come full circle. ExxonMobil was replicating the scale and dominance of its distant ancestor Standard Oil.

ExxonMobil's success was built by its CEO, Lee Raymond, whose titanic drive matched that of Rockefeller. A chemical engineer, Raymond replicated Rockefeller's stinginess and relentless commitment to operational efficiency.

Exxon's employees had a cult-like conformity. According to *Private Empire* by Steve Coll, the employees were expected to marry, be practising Protestants and to avoid vices. They were defined by the motto, "We don't smoke; we don't chew; we don't hang out with those who do".

Exxon hired the cream of the US' engineering talent. The objective was to operate the business with the lowest costs, irrespective of the cycle. The company's overarching aims were twofold. First, fossil fuels would remain the principal energy source. Second, Exxon would go to any length to find and sell new oil and gas reserves.

As with all energy companies, Exxon is required to report its energy reserves to the Securities and Exchange Commission annually. This is a formidable task for American companies. Much of the world's oil is in the hands of hostile regimes. They include Iran, Venezuela and Iraq.

ExxonMobil chose a novel and bold path. Instead of focusing on the known oil producers, it sought oil in obscure countries—Equatorial Guinea, Chad and Nigeria. This strategy was dangerous, as contracts are poorly enforced in these countries. They are also riven by coups and wars. There is the risk of the violating of US laws in countries where corruption is the norm.

Despite these obstacles, ExxonMobil has established a vice-like grip on energy supplies in these countries. In 2001, Equatorial Guinea contributed 8% of ExxonMobil's oil and gas production. The MNC had negotiated a lucrative contract with the country's regime and paid royalties of only 10%.

The twin pillars of cutting costs and replenishing oil reserves have defined the company. The commodity collapse places ExxonMobil at the low ebb of its 10-year valuation range on a price-to-free-cash-flow basis. ExxonMobil's free cash flow is secure and sufficient to meet its dividend yield of 3%.

In the wake of the oil price collapse, Exxon cut its capital and cash operating costs by $11.5 billion ($15.8 billion) last year. This helped the company improve its gross margin profile in the oil price rout.

ExxonMobil is the king of the oil trade. Its dividends are the diamonds on its crown. Investors should not wallow in the commodity cycle, but bet on a company that has stood firm.

Postscript

ExxonMobil has fallen in line with commodity prices. Its earnings have been relatively steady. The shift away from resources has hurt the stock price.

Total Return

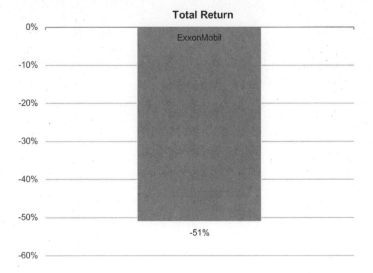

EMERGING
MARKETS

What stocks to buy post-Castro's Cuba?

Published on December 19, 2016

Fidel Castro, Cuba's brutal dictator, died on November 25. Coincidentally, he came to power in 1959, the same year that the People's Action Party, led by Lee Kuan Yew, first took office in Singapore.

Remarkably, Cuba's GDP per capita was three times higher than Singapore's in 1959. Havana, Cuba's capital, was a playground of the US elite. Its casinos and tourist hotels made it the Miami of its time.

Singapore was a colonial outpost burdened with violence and hardship. It had few natural resources. Cuba had a major tobacco, sugar and coffee industry. Cuban cigars were a global luxury.

Fifty-seven years later, Singapore's GDP per capita is 10 times that of Cuba's. Cuba's roads are potholed and its citizens drive antique vehicles. Food shortages are endemic.

Singapore, on the other hand, is an international financial centre that matches New York and London. It has more millionaires per capita than any other country, as well as 100 times Cuba's foreign reserves.

The divergence between these two tropical islands is because Singapore embraced the free market. Cuba was engulfed by communism. Responsible fiscal management, free trade and strong property rights are at the heart of Singapore's transformation. Cuba wiped out free enterprise and restricted economic freedoms.

Since 1959, Singapore's per capita income has grown 118-fold. Cuba's living standards are lower today than they were in 1991, when its benefactor, the Soviet Union, collapsed. The poverty rate is 26%. The economy is facing bankruptcy and a balance-of-payment crisis.

Capitalism requires the rule of law. Like the US, Singapore has a robust legal regime based on English common law. Singapore is consistently among the top-ranked countries in the world in ease of doing business.

Cuba under Castro and his brother Raul has virtually wiped out free enterprise. It is the least free economy in the Western Hemisphere.

With Castro's death, there is a ray of hope. In fact, Raul has initiated some market reforms. This is an unmitigated relief to Cuba's long-suffering people. The country has the ingredients of a post-communist export powerhouse, such as China and Vietnam. Its workers are skilled, it is at the US' doorstep and its wages are competitive. The country also has vast mineral reserves and an advanced biotech industry.

Raul has already taken infant steps to reverse his brother's disastrous policies. In 2014, Cuba passed foreign investment laws. He created a special economic development zone, modelled on China's special economic zone, in Mariel Bay. Labour laws would be relaxed in this zone. The government plans to dismantle and reform the state-owned enterprises that are chronically inefficient.

Cuba's giant neighbour has taken note. In the last few years, the US has begun to remove its stringent sanction regime. For instance, US banks can handle Cuban transactions and US companies can open offices, warehouses and shops in Cuba.

The stock market proxies for Cuba require some digging. There are a handful of international companies that have circumvented the sanctions. These include Spain's **Meliá Hotels International** and Canada's **Sherritt International**.

Almost a tenth of Meliá Hotels International's earnings are derived from Cuba and the ratio could double.

Sherritt International is by far the largest investor in Cuba. It operates oil and gas plants and mines cobalt and nickel. The stock has long traded at a discount to its peers, which may be unwarranted.

Economic activity has been suppressed in Cuba. A construction boom is likely to accompany the liberalisation. There is a craving for affordable housing. **Vulcan Materials Co.**, the largest producer of building materials in the US, runs a massive quarry in Mexico in the Yucatan Peninsula, which is ideally placed to export to Cuba.

The stock seems highly priced at 43 times FY2017 earnings, but is expected to generate 65% earnings growth.

In fact, Mexican companies would be Cuba plays. **América Móvil**, **Cemex** and **Coca-Cola Femsa** seem on the verge of expanding in Cuba. Mexican companies may have the stomach for Cuba's volatile retreat from communism owing to the cultural links.

Castro often said "a revolution is not a bed of roses" when confronted with the hardship of his people. Cuba's investment prospects are rosy with his passing.

Postscript

Castro's death was a signal moment for Cuba-related stocks. They have all rallied as Cuba's isolation has eased.

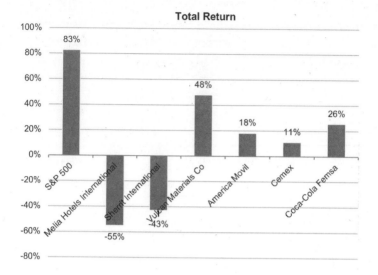

Total Return

- S&P 500: 83%
- Melia Hotels International: -55%
- Sherit International: -43%
- Vulcan Materials Co: 48%
- America Movil: 18%
- Cemex: 11%
- Coca-Cola Femsa: 26%

As Thailand grieves, three winning stocks ensure Teflon economy continues

Published on November 7, 2016

Thailand's King Bhumibol Adulyadej, who died recently at the age of 88, was born 11 years before the invention of Teflon, the indestructible chemical compound that can withstand high temperatures. During his 70-year reign, Thailand became known as the Teflon economy.

Thailand was a poor rural economy when the king was crowned in 1946, but today it is a modern economy. Its income per capita has risen 95 times during the king's reign. Its stock market has risen threefold since foreign investment was allowed in 1987. Its economy has weathered severe storms, including 12 coups and a harrowing economic crisis in 1997. Tourists and investors have flocked to the kingdom, famed for its lush beaches and lavish hospitality. The king was a stabiliser and unifier. He eased tensions between the military and civilian politicians.

Secret sauce

What was the secret sauce that made the king a source of stability? The king had been at the centre of Thailand's success. The monarch had a symbolic value well beyond his formal powers. He was a potent icon of defiance in a country that was never colonised. Various military governments actually raised his stature. General Sarit Thanarat, a military ruler in the 1960s, revived practices such as prostrating before royalty.

The king also extended his authority through the Privy

Council. The Privy Council was the centre of a network with the king at the fulcrum, with a wide ambit that includes politics and business. It plays a vital role particularly during a vacuum.

King Bhumibol was the richest monarch in the world with an estimated fortune of US$30 billion ($41.6 billion). Despite his fabled wealth, he passionately advocated the cause of the poor. This endeared him to the masses.

Some investors fear that his death has come at a time of trouble. Since the military coup of May 2014, civilian politics has come to a standstill. Dissidents have been arrested. This year's referendum passed a constitution that essentially enthroned the military.

However, King Bhumibol's successor, Crown Prince Maha Vajiralongkorn, inherits an institution that is likely to maintain Thailand's stability. The Privy Council and the widespread popularity of the royal family are intact.

Blue-chip stocks

Thailand's Teflon quality is seen in the resilience of its blue-chip stocks. There are three stocks that stand out for their ability to withstand severe pressure. The first is **Thai Beverage**, the country's third largest company by market capitalisation. It is listed in Singapore but its operations are largely in Thailand.

ThaiBev has the potential to become one of Southeast Asia's few MNCs. It is controlled by the Charoen Sirivadhanabhakdi family, which has entrenched itself in the liquor business for decades. Their genius lies in branding and distribution.

ThaiBev has long had a vice-like grip on Thailand's spirits market. Spirits make up over 85% of its profits. It also controls the Chang beer brand, which sponsors the Everton football team.

The company is in the unique position of generating earnings growth when consumer spending sinks. People drink in good times, as well as bad times. In 2014, consumer spending fell sharply, but ThaiBev recorded handsome profits. Its associate stake in **Fraser and Neave**, a regional beverage giant, places it on a pedestal for regional expansion.

Charoen Pokphand Foods is another consumer stock with global aspirations. Through a series of judicious acquisitions, CPF is now Asia's biggest meat company. It produces feed for chickens and pigs, along with branded meat products. Asia's hunger for protein means that meat will be at the forefront of consumer choice. As countries become more prosperous, meat consumption accelerates.

Like Thailand, CPF has bounced back from adversity. In 2006, its operating profits fell 67% due to bird flu. There was a mass slaughter of livestock. However, by 2008, CPF had completely recovered. Since, then CPF (and its chickens) have been flying high. It has recorded an earnings compound annual growth rate of 21%.

Another Thai jewel is **Minor International**, a hospitality company founded in 1978 by an American, Bill Heinecke. It operates 150 hotels and 1,800 restaurants in over 10 countries, applying Thai hospitality practices to the rest of the region. The diversity of its leisure offerings means that it can withstand travel disruptions. For instance, the losses from a terrorist attack in Bali would be offset by increased traffic to Sri Lanka.

Investors and the grief-stricken Thai public should not despair. There should be a platform for stability if the monarchy's authority is maintained. Investing in these three winners may even outlast Teflon.

Postscript

The Thai stocks have performed badly five years after the King's demise. The tourism-reliant economy has been hit hard by the pandemic. CPF and Minor International are sufficiently nimble to bounce back.

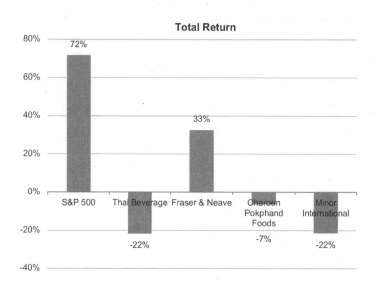

Are emerging markets about to turn around?

Published on September 23, 2016

Do you remember 1981? It was the year Prince Charles and Lady Diana were married, and the IBM PC was introduced. Few would remember that it was also the year the term "emerging market was coined.

The credit for this marketing masterstroke lies with an erudite Dutchman called Antoine van Agtmael. He was deputy director of International Finance Corp, the investment arm of the World Bank. The then 34-year-old van Agtmael had just returned from a stint in Thailand, where he was struck by its vibrant economic prospects. However, the stock market valuations of Thailand and other poor countries were unjustly low.

He suggested that Salomon Brothers create a "Third-World Equity Fund". Salomon rejected the Third World moniker, finding it negative, and sought an uplifting term. Van Agtmael suggested "emerging markets", and the term caught on like wildfire.

Emerging markets have since risen to be a major asset class. An emerging markets fund was launched by Capital International in 1986 with US$50 million. Today, American investors alone have more than US$420 billion ($566.2 billion) in emerging markets.

Six years after the coinage, van Agtmael founded an investment firm called Emerging Markets Management. Its assets under management peaked at US$20 billion. Van Agtmael and his partners disposed of their stake to Ashmore Group in 2011 for more than US$126 million.

The disposal seems well-timed. Today, the sentiment towards emerging markets is emphatically negative. Investors fear an emerging market meltdown. A recent survey found that one third of institutional investors felt an emerging markets crisis was the largest risk.

The fears are due to the huge volatility in China's stock market and the collapse in commodity prices. Yet Brazil and Russia, two countries suffering from the slump in commodity prices, have been among the best performers in the world in 2016.

Could other depressed emerging markets be about to stage big rebounds? Are investors just too negative on these markets?

Price-to-book (P/B) ratios are an excellent way of valuing emerging market equities. They eliminate the subjectivity of both forward and historical earnings. A company's book value is simply the total value of its assets that shareholders may theoretically receive in liquidation.

The P/B ratio of the MSCI Emerging Markets index is 1.4 times today. This means that if a company were to go bankrupt, its investors would receive 70% of their investment. This valuation is among the lowest since the index was introduced in 1989. In the last 27 years, the valuation has been lower on only two occasions.

Both occasions were unmitigated buying opportunities. They were the 1997/98 Asian financial crisis, when the valuation reached 0.94 times and briefly after Sept 11, 2001, when it touched 1.1 times. The MSCI EM index rose 31% and 39% in the six months following the two respective lows. At 1.2 times P/B, the chances of success are high. The average 12-month return for investing at 1.2 times P/B has been more than 40%.

The parallels with the 1997/98 crisis are tenuous.

Emerging market economies, particularly in Asia, are nowhere as indebted as they were then. In the last decade, Malaysia's private-debt-to-GDP ratio has risen 19%. India's has risen 17% and Indonesia's 13%. In the decade prior to the 1997 collapse, the private-debt to-GDP ratio rose 50% in Malaysia and 100% in Thailand.

There was a basic currency mismatch in those dark days. The Asian economies had borrowed heavily in foreign currency, leaving themselves vulnerable to depreciation. In a famous example, the Steady Safe taxi company in Jakarta had US$265 million in US dollar debt, while its revenues were entirely in rupiah.

Today, these economies have curbed excessive foreign borrowing and amassed massive amounts of foreign reserves. In fact, the total foreign reserves of emerging markets are in excess of developed markets.

The clincher in favour of emerging market equities are the record-low bond yields in the developed world. There is now a pool of US$13 trillion of negative yield bonds in the West and Japan. Emerging markets, where dividend and bond yields are at least four times higher, need to be placed on a pedestal.

Van Agtmael prospered from a unique mix of marketing and investing. Investors should dive into this asset class as it seems better placed now than at any point since his moment of inspiration in 1981.

Postscript

Emerging Market equities have been the poor relation in the great stock market boom of the last five years. The S&P500 has doubled the performance of Emerging Markets. Tech represents more than half the rise in S&P500. Emerging Markets have far less technology exposure.

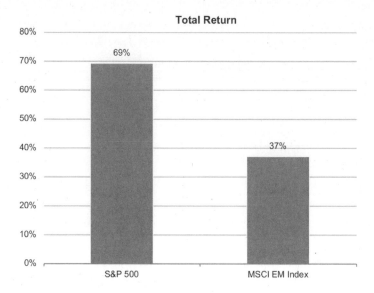

Total Return

Why Bangladesh still beckons despite its troubles

Published on July 12, 2016

The name "Bangladesh" shot to fame in August 1971 with a rock concert in New York's Madison Square Garden. Bangladesh was then a part of Pakistan and was ravaged by a savage, separatist war. The concert raised funds for the conflict's 10 million refugees.

Over 40,000 people gyrated to Bob Dylan, Eric Clapton and the Indian maestro Ravi Shankar. Not only did they raise US$250,000 (US$1.5m in today's terms), but an obscure backwater became a household name. Ravi Shankar would later recall that "In one day, the whole world knew the name of Bangladesh. It was a fantastic occasion…"

Today, the country evokes fear and not sympathy. Last week's appalling massacre of foreign visitors in the Bangladeshi capital of Dhaka is the latest in a series of atrocities. Since 2015, there have been attacks on intellectuals, religious moderates and minorities. The recent victims include Italians, Japanese, Indians and an American. Bangladesh is now classed along with Iraq, Algeria and other countries facing Islamist terror.

The Dhaka Stock Exchange, one of the top frontier markets, has swooned 30% in the face of violence. The government bond market has fallen 25%.

The retreat from this frontier market is unwarranted. Bangladesh has enticing prospects to join Asia's Tiger economies in a generation. It has a population of over 169 million and an income per capita that is an eighth of that of

China. This means that it has some of the lowest labour costs in the world.

With its vast reserves of cheap labour, Bangladesh's principle industry is the US$26 billion garment industry. Over four million people are employed in this industry. They are mostly rural women, who earn about US$3 a day.

Top brands such as Marks & Spencer, Gap and Next are produced in Bangladesh. The country has carved a world-class niche. Bangladesh is highly efficient in an industry with high barriers to entry. The listed proxies for this include **Adamjee Jute Mills** and **Ha-meem Group**.

Clothes produced by cheap factory workers are not the only opportunity. Bangladesh has a vibrant financial sector that is at the cutting edge of fintech. Only 15% of the population have a bank account. But, mobile phone penetration is over 70%. **BRAC Bank**, a bank that emanated from NGO, has created one of the world's largest mobile payment markets. According to Bloomberg consensus, earnings growth could exceed 25% a year. The Bank is trading at a price to book of just 1.2x.

Almost a tenth of Bangladesh's US$150 billion GDP consists of remittances from foreign workers. Bangladesh is a major supplier of construction labour in the Gulf and Southeast Asia. There are also engineers and doctors in the West, as well as technicians.

The upshot of this remittance flow is a rapid consumer boom in a poor country. In 2004, I visited Dhaka for the first time. The decaying streets were clogged with cycle rickshaws and pedestrians. Dhotis (subcontinental sarongs) were the principal male attire. There were only two hotels in the city that served international visitors. The better restaurants mainly catered to Western aid workers.

Things were different when I visited last year. The cycle

rickshaws have been replaced by auto rickshaws. There are now 10 luxury hotels in Dhaka. The restaurants served business travellers, as well as prosperous locals. Many of the pedestrians had discarded dhotis and wore trendy blazers and trousers in the subcontinental winter.

The impact of the remittance flow is strongest at the bottom of the pyramid. Only 7% of the country's population are classed by the World Bank as middle class, compared to 38% in Indonesia. The average daily income in Bangladesh is US$3. The companies that will benefit from the consumer boom are the ones that sell ordinary items such as a shampoo, hair oil, and snacks.

Marico, the country's largest hair oil producer, prices its products as low as US$1.50 a unit. They use small packaging to tap the vast market of poor consumers.

Foreigners can open an account in Bangladeshi brokerages. However, it can be cumbersome to monitor. There is a Bangladeshi ETF listed in Singapore that tracks the **DSE** (MSCI Bangladesh IM Index UCITS ETF 1C), which may be an ideal proxy. At 14x and 6% dividend yield, it compares favourably with most frontier markets.

As the massacres in Texas and France show, Bangladesh does not have a monopoly on violence. The country has been resilient amidst poverty, floods and violence. Investors need to drill behind the headlines and dance to the tune that Bob Dylan sang in the summer of 1971.

Postscript

Bangladesh's stock market has floundered, despite its high economic growth. This is part of the general retreat from the illiquid frontier markets to the roaring technology stocks in the US.

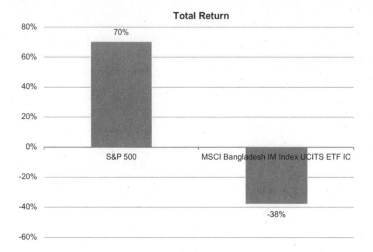

The exotic appeal of frontier bonds

Published on June 6, 2016

The stench of rotting tuna can be unbearable. It can also be distracting. This year, Mozambique's tuna bond has caused a big stink for the frontier bond market.

In 2013, Mozambique raised US$850 million for its state-owned tuna fishing company Ematum. The funds were raised for "tuna fishing and related infrastructure". However, the Mozambicans used US$500 million for defence. Only US$350 million was used for tuna fishing. Now, the Mozambicans are struggling to repay it. They are trying to force a restructuring. This has outraged investors and increased fears over frontier bonds.

But the stench of tuna should not detract from the appeal of this sweet-smelling asset class. Though they are shunned by investors deterred by "Third World" woes, frontier bonds have vastly outperformed developed market debt since the turn of the millennium.

Frontier markets were coined by the IFC in 1992 to describe poor economies that are too small to be an emerging market. They include countries such as Angola, Sri Lanka, Kenya and Pakistan. These countries have favourable growth prospects but are less integrated with global finance. MSCI classifies 26 countries as frontier markets.

Since 2008, there has been an explosion of frontier market sovereign bond issues. It peaked in 2014, when US$23 billion was issued. The hunger for yield has been driven by record-low interest rates in the West. It has also been driven by the desire of frontier economies to move beyond foreign aid.

Over the last decade, countries ranging from Ivory Coast to Sri Lanka have tapped the sovereign bond market. These countries typically have a credit rating that is below investment grade. There has been a four-fold rise in foreign investment in the frontier market local-currency bond market.

In fact, frontier sovereign debt has been the best performing of the global fixed income asset classes over the last 12 months. Actually, frontier market sovereign debt has been the best performing fixed income asset class since the turn of the millennium.

The frontier sovereign credit market has returned 9%, versus to 2% for the US Treasury index in the last year. The US junk bond market has returned -4 % for junk corporate bonds.

Since January 2001, frontier bonds have had a cumulative return of 310%. The US investment-grade corporate bonds have returned just 170%. Despite recovering from the depths of the tech bubble, NASDAQ has only returned 168% in that period. S&P500 has returned 119%.

The value of frontier market sovereign bonds and local currency bonds is built on three pillars. First, frontier bonds can offer investors better returns compared to mainstream emerging market bonds with less volatility. Frontier markets are a worthy investment. Investors are adequately compensated for the risks.

The Sharpe Ratio is an indication of the risk-adjusted return of an asset. The higher the Sharpe Ratio, the better the risk-adjusted return. From 2004 to 2014, frontier market bonds have generated better Sharpe Ratios (0.56) than Emerging Market Equities (0.36) and Developed Market Sovereign Debt (0.33).

Second, frontier bonds have low correlation to US treasuries. Frontier markets are obscure. Many American fund managers will be hard-pressed to find Mozambique on the map, let alone comment on its tuna industry. Over the last decade, the correlation coefficient between frontier market bonds and US treasury has been negligible, at just 0.06. In fact, frontier market bonds gained due to the global financial crisis.

Finally, there are very few indices that track frontier bonds. Neither the sovereign nor corporate market has generated many indices. The main option for investors is to take a direct position.

2016 has witnessed the dawn of a novel concept in finance – negative interest rates. In Japan and Europe, depositors are actually charged to keep their money in an account. Several European central banks have cut interest rates to below zero.

Last week, Sri Lanka's Governor of the Central Bank Arjuna Mahendran made a forceful case for his economy at the Sri Lanka Investment Summit in Singapore. The oil price collapse has boosted current account balance much more than portfolio investment.

The anomaly of negative interest rates presents an opportunity. It means that one can borrow at -1% in Europe or Japan and invest in Sri Lanka's 10-year bond which yields 12%. This would generate an effective return of 13%. S&P rates Sri Lanka just below investment grade at B+. A credit upgrade from the oil price collapse could turbocharge the bond market.

Like Mozambique, Sri Lanka depends on fishing. However, Sri Lanka's bonds and others in its asset class have an enticing fragrance that may drown out the stench of Mozambican tuna.

Postscript

Despite the high yields, frontier and emerging market bonds returns have not matched S&P500. The returns have been steady but unspectacular. There could be a rotation in their favour, as US interest rates are at record lows.

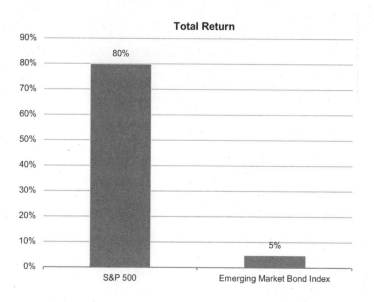

Total Return

Financial trouble at India's UB Group turns spotlight on looming NPL crisis

Published on February 29, 2016

When I met Vijay Mallya in 2008, he struck me as energetic and witty. A chain-smoker who donned gold jewellery, he had the manner of a pop singer rather than a tycoon. The brash image served him well. Mallya is CEO of United Breweries Group (UB Group), which produces Kingfisher beer. Being known as the "King of Good Times" was an inspired marketing tactic.

The problem is that Mallya also steered UB Group into launching an airline, a business that suited his outsized ego more than the profitability of the company. In 2012, Kingfisher Airlines halted operations after its licence was revoked. Kingfisher Airlines now owes some US$1.1 billion to 17 banks. In late April, India revoked Mallya's passport after he was alleged to have fled the country to avoid legal action by creditors, some of whom have declared him "a wilful defaulter".

Mallya has been defiant. In an interview with the *Financial Times*, he blamed his difficulties on greedy bankers and the media frenzy over his financial difficulties. He claims that his lenders were fully aware of the financial position of Kingfisher Airlines. It faced high fuel prices. He also says that banks are now reluctant to take a haircut on his obligations because of his high profile.

The travails of UB Group are a microcosm of a brewing bad loan crisis in India. Unless urgent action is taken, a tsunami of defaults may besiege this vast nation. India's economy has suffered a slowdown in industrial activity and faltering foreign direct investment. Non-performing loans in the country have tripled in the last four years.

A non-performing loan is one that ceases generating income for a bank for more than 90 days. A slice of this typically ends up being unrecoverable. India's NPLs are currently about 5% of the country's gross loans, a ratio that is some three times that of China. India's net NPL ratio is 14% of net loans, or some US$131 billion. Credit Suisse has estimated that this figure may rise to 18% over the next few years.

What does this mean for India's banks? The governor of the Reserve Bank of India Raghuram Rajan has reached for medical analogies. He has called for "deep surgery" on the balance sheets of banks. Recognising and writing off bad loans hits the profitability of banks. But it could force them to raise more capital. It puts them in better shape to lend to new businesses and support an economic recovery.

India could look to this region for a model to handle a bad debt crisis. In 1997, the collapse of currencies like the Thai baht, Indonesian rupiah and Malaysian ringgit sparked a massive recession. The NPL ratio in some ASEAN countries soared to well over 40%, way beyond even the most bearish forecasts for India. Indonesia was the worst hit. By January 1998, the rupiah had depreciated 87%. In US dollar terms, the market value of Jakarta-listed companies had shrunk to less than 7% of their July 1997 level.

Yet, the recovery was as dramatic as the collapse. With the slump in their currencies, ASEAN countries suddenly became highly competitive exporters. They also took proactive steps to fix their banks. In January 1998, Indonesia also created a special agency—Indonesian Bank Restructuring Agency—to dispose of the bad debts.

This agency relieved the banks of their toxic assets and

provided liquidity for these distressed assets. Indonesia's economy quickly recovered. By 2011, the market value of Jakarta-listed companies returned to their 1997 peak levels in US dollar terms.

Today, the balance sheets of ASEAN banks are more secure. It is also much easier to recover NPLs due to legal reforms. Even with slowing economic growth and the slump in oil prices, NPLs are now well below 10%.

Tycoons like Mallya are derided by India's public. Even as his UB Group has struggled with debt, the businessman has continued living the high life. In November, he celebrated his 60th birthday in lavish style, complete with free-flowing champagne and a performance by Julio Iglesias. While the employees of Kingfisher Airlines have gone unpaid, Mallya himself recently claimed US$75 million for relinquishing the post of chairman of a unit the group sold to Diageo in 2012.

Prince, the master lyricist of the 1980s, who died last month as Mallya's corporate empire was collapsing, said it best in the hit song 1999: "Life is just a party and parties weren't meant to last."

Postscript

India's banking crisis has weighed on the stock market. Its returns have not matched the S&P500.

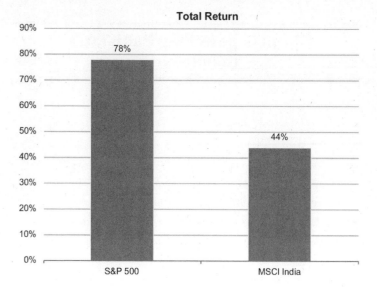

Total Return

China is powering Pakistan's turnaround

Published on June 6, 2016

Appearances are deceptive. Pakistan is viewed as a backwater riven by violence. The gory images of the Easter Sunday massacre in Lahore have monopolized headlines. Violence, mostly from Taliban-linked insurgents who want to impose their perverse version of Islam, has killed 60,000 people in the last 15 years.

However, the real story in this country with a larger population than Russia is vastly different. Pakistan is not the only country riven by terrorism. It is a captivating investment destination that is on the cusp of rapid growth. In fact, its stock market is among the best positioned frontier markets.

It has been over seven years since the restoration of civilian rule. Pakistan's civilian rulers are not angelic. However, civilian rule has lessened the war-like approach of Pakistan's military.

Many countries have a military. But, Pakistan has the only military with a country! The military budget is US$7.4 billion. However, the Pakistani military's private business empire could be worth almost three times that amount. Pakistan's officers run industrial conglomerates. They manufacture products ranging from cement to cereal. They own 12 million acres of public land.

The military has ruled for about half of Pakistan's history since independence. They have fought four wars against Pakistan's existential foe, India. The military has spearheaded a proxy war in Afghanistan. Happily, the military's largesse has distracted them from intervening in politics since 2008.

Relations with India have improved since Mr Nawaz Sharif returned to office in 2013. Mr Sharif has been Prime Minister twice before. He is emphatically pro-business and was at the forefront of the privatisation programme in the 1990s. Mr Sharif is also a religious conservative backed by the Islamic lobby.

His conservatism is matched by his counterparts across the border. India is headed by the Hindu nationalist Bharatiya Janata Party of Narendra Modi. Both governments are secure in their milieu and are intent on dialogue. This is fortuitous for Pakistan.

China is pivotal to the US$270 billion economy's emergence. Mr Sharif is boosting infrastructure with support from China and the IMF. Infrastructure shortages have throttled Pakistan's growth.

China has stepped in to fill the gaping hole, particularly in the power industry. Massive investments have boosted Pakistan's FDI in the last year. Last year, Pakistan received 39 green field investments totalling US$18.9 billion, representing 148% Y-O-Y rise. Most of the investment was from China.

China has overtaken UAE as the country's top investor. China's Shanghai Electric, a power generator, is building a 1,320 megawatt coal-based power project in Tharparkar. Power and energy was over 65% of the FDI into Pakistan last year. The transport sector is another major area of investment, with 12 projects amounting to US$3 billion last year.

Pakistan's chronic disability has been its reliance on imported energy. The oil price collapse from US$140/barrel to US$40/barrel is a godsend for Pakistan. Oil imports are a third of Pakistan's total imports. The country's petroleum import bill in 2015/16 may be half of the level in 2013/14. Pakistan's current account deficit has fallen by 49% Y-O-Y to just 0.5% of GDP. Foreign reserves are solid at US$22 billion.

Pakistan is one of the few markets with a buoyant IPO market. The steel sector, which is a direct beneficiary of the infrastructure upgrade, is prominent among the listings. Amreli Steels Ltd raised $36 millon in an IPO to double its capacity. Mughal Iron & Steel Industries IPO was 25 times oversubscribed.

Cement, another infrastructure related sector, is on the move. DG Khan Cement Co. controlled by billionaire Mian Muhammad Mansha and Cherat Cement Co are doubling their capacity.

The infrastructure expansion provides fuel to Pakistan's nascent export sector. At US$29 billion, exports are just 11% of GDP. This is a fraction of the export contribution in the ASEAN economies. Pakistan's exports such as textiles, wheat and cotton are likely to surge as the shackles of poor infrastructure are released.

Frontier markets like Pakistan have limited correlation with traditional asset classes such as developed markets and emerging markets. In the last five years, Pakistan's main equity index has outperformed the S&P500 by a factor of 2.5 times.

At 8x FY16 earnings, Pakistan's market is trading at 70% to the MSCI Asia PE. At 3%, its dividend yield is enticing.

Investing directly in Pakistan's stock market is cumbersome. Many people view Pakistan as isolated. Actually, there is a Pakistan ETF which trades in Singapore – DB X-Trackers **MSCI Pakistan**. As with the security situation, Pakistan's rosy reality radically differs from its perception.

Postscript

Pakistan's stock market has been weak, despite the allure of its economy. As a frontier market, it has been ignored in the face of the tech boom in the US.

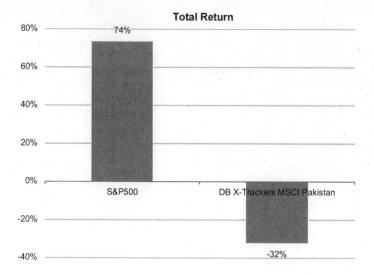

How cheap oil is a boon for India

Published on January 27, 2016

The world is awash with oil. Brent crude prices have fallen 75% from the summer of 2014. They are at their lowest ebb since 2003. The suddenness of the decline has been a curse for oil producing countries and oil majors. Saudi Arabia needs oil prices to be at US$100 a barrel to balance its budget. Russia faces mass unemployment. Even with a dividend yield of 9%, BP's shares are floundering.

One man's misery is another man's fortune. Low oil prices are creating a bonanza for India, which imports 80% of its oil. High oil prices in the last decade was a huge contributor to the chronic current account deficit. India's oil import bill also dwarfed its spending on infrastructure, health and education.

Now, the oil collapse is having a greater impact on its balance payments than foreign portfolio investment. In 2014, India saved US$25 billion on oil imports, which is almost twice the country's portfolio investment. Last year, the figure swelled to US$55 billion. If oil prices stay at present levels, India could soon wipe out its current account deficit. Portfolio investment would become less relevant in the face of the oil bonanza.

Meanwhile, cheaper oil is spurring consumer spending in India. It has driven the World Bank's upgrade of its GDP growth from 7.5% in 2015 to 7.9% in 2016. Every dollar drop in oil prices cuts fuel subsidy payments by $1 billion. Consumers also have more money in their pockets.

It is sweetening the bitter pill of reform. Since independence, India has been a capitalist society that has been shackled by a socialist state. In May 2014, Narendra Modi, a free market reformer, was elected. He set about slashing the government's large fuel subsidies. Before Modi's election, India had fuel subsidies of almost $22 billion for consumers. Much of that has been cut.

If oil prices continue falling, India could now be in a good position to deregulate fuel prices entirely. Indian consumers would benefit significantly from this. Oil prices may have dropped by 75% in the last 18 months, but the petrol at the pump has fallen by just 17%.

The oil collapse not only redistributes income between oil producers and importers. It disproportionately benefits the consumer at the bottom of the pyramid, as opposed to the middle classes. India's constitutional commitment to socialism may be finally being realized.

The effects of stronger consumer spending are already apparent. **Eicher Motors**, a motorcycle manufacturer, recorded 59% Y-O-Y growth in 2015. Motorcycles with less than 350cc engine capacity are favoured by poorer customers. These are typically pioneering buyers who are graduating from a bicycle to a motorcycle. Sales of these bikes grew 63% to 40,280 units from 24,662. The larger models with over 350cc engine capacity sold a quarter more at 4,211 units compared to 3,358 last year.

The real fortune is even further down the pyramid. The poor tend to be affected much more by commodity price cycles. With lower fuel prices, companies selling basic items to the poor will find a new lease of life in India.

Hindustan Unilever, the FMCG giant whose sales represent 2% of India's GDP, has mastered selling to the common man. They target the poor by taking lower margins for their basic products. They can compensate for this by pricing shampoo for the prosperous customers at a premium.

Hindustan Unilever sells Lux shampoo in fancy packaging, as well as in simple sachets.

In rural India, the sale of another oil is booming – hair oil. This product is often the first cosmetic product used by the rural poor. Marico is the leader in that field. A typical bottle of hair oil sells for less than US$2. In 1HFY15, Marico's hair oil sales grew by 14%, driving a 22% jump in operating profits.

The plague of locusts ravaging the oil industry may pave the way for prosperity. India is on the cusp of a consumer boom that investors cannot ignore.

Postscript

India has rallied on the back of cheap oil. Low oil prices have done more for India's economy than foreign investment.

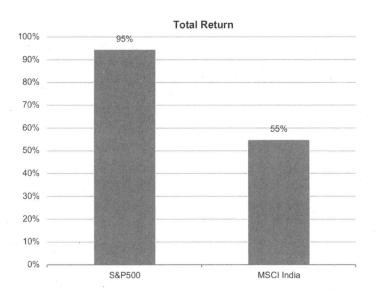

Three lessons for ASEAN from the life of former Singapore DPM S. Rajaratnam

Published on December 18, 2015

This years' New Year revelry will have a special resonance for ASEAN's 600 million people. On 31st December 2015, ASEAN is set to create the ASEAN Economic Community (AEC). The AEC will oblige the 10 member nations to create a single market, inspired by the European Union. The aim is to have a free flow of services, investment, labour and capital.

The latest addition to the alphabet soup of regional groupings has immense prospects. ASEAN was created in 1967 as a US-inspired bulwark against communism in this region. The Cold War ended 25 years ago, but ASEAN's economic integration is yet to be fully realized.

The AEC should seek inspiration from the life of Sinnathamby Rajaratnam, one of ASEAN's founding fathers. Rajaratnam was born 100 years ago in the northern part of Ceylon (now Sri Lanka). His family was settled in British Malaya, where his father was a minor executive in a rubber estate. Rajaratnam studied law in London in the 1940s. The Second World War prevented him from completing his studies. He returned to British Malaya, which then included Singapore, and worked as a journalist before entering politics.

Rajaratnam had a titanic drive and immersed himself in Malaya's independence struggle. When Singapore suddenly split from Malaysia in 1965, he became the city-state's Minister of Foreign Affairs. He later rose to be Deputy Prime Minister. On the 100th anniversary of his birth, as well as Singapore's

50th anniversary as an independent country, Rajaratnam provides three vital lessons for AEC.

Free trade is the only way. During ASEAN's inception, most Third World countries were pursuing import substitution industrialization (ISI). In the 1960s, over 95% of the consumer goods in Peru, Brazil and Mexico were supplied domestically. India had an average tariff rate of over 600% at one point during a dark era known as the Licence Raj.

By the sharpest of contrasts, the ASEAN countries adopted low tariffs. Rajaratnam was a trenchant advocate of free trade. He encouraged ASEAN to pursue free trade agreements, when such arrangements were derided. That resulted in Indonesia, Thailand and Malaysia becoming the workshop of the world. They exploited their comparative advantage to pursue export-oriented liberalization. Malaysia's GDP per capita has grown 30-fold since 1967, while India's has grown just 15-fold.

AEC is the culmination of Rajaratnam's passion for free trade. There is a long list of items that would be subject to the AEC's tariff-free regime. Intra-ASEAN trade is just 25% of total trade in the region, but this figure will rise. A unified market for goods and services is upon us.

Rajaratnam had a reverence for education. Rajaratnam was the only Singaporean cabinet minister without a degree, but he was the most erudite. His conversations were littered with allusions to the classics. As Labour Minister, he was instrumental in transforming the quality of Singapore's workforce.

In 1966, more than half of Singaporean workers had absolutely no formal education. Today, Singapore has universal secondary education. Over a sixth of people have a university degree. The country has two universities that are ranked among the 100 best universities in the world.

The divergence with India is striking. In India, only 40% of the population have secondary education. Despite having 1.3 billion people, not a single Indian university has been ranked as one of the world's 100 best universities.

ASEAN's economic outperformance may have been driven by superior education. Since 1967, ASEAN economies have grown at an average of 6%, which is faster than any other regional grouping.

Rajaratnam embraced diversity long before its importance was recognized. His family's prospects were allied to the British Empire's cosmopolitanism. The British Empire opened up employment opportunities for ambitious and talented people like Rajaratnam's father. He was born into a Hindu family and married a Hungarian Christian named Piroska Feher whom he met in London. When Rajaratnam authored Singapore's national pledge in 1966, he committed the citizens to work together despite racial and religious differences.

ASEAN was built on the bedrock of non-interference in the domestic affairs of its member states. Its members have enjoyed harmony despite including Catholic-majority Philippines, Buddhist Thailand and Muslim-dominated Indonesia. As AEC emerges, consensual decisions will be vital to accommodate diversity.

Investors in emerging markets have been besotted and burnt by the BRIC nations of Brazil, Russia, India and China. ASEAN, a region that embraced capitalism before the BRICs, is on the brink of a renewal. Investors ignore AEC at their peril.

Postscript

ASEAN has had a torrid time as the pandemic has hit it hard. Also, it has less technology exposure compared to the roaring US markets.

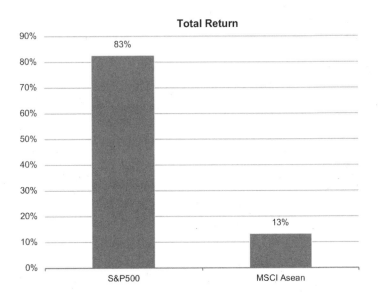

Will ASEAN's dalliance with debt spark another financial crisis?

Published on December 13, 2015

Cocktails are all the rage in Singapore's bars, after long being dominated by whisky. Meanwhile, a cocktail of ambition, debt and inertia threatens to create a hangover in ASEAN.

Back in 1997, when indebted corporates faced weakening currencies, the region suffered a debilitating crisis. In 1999, economists Barry Eichengreen and Ricardo Hausmann applied the term "original sin" to the difficulty faced by emerging markets in borrowing overseas in their own currencies. They also suggested that it was hard for borrowers in these countries to even obtain long-term domestic debt.

There are ominous signs of a repeat. With US interest rates at record lows, ASEAN has been on a credit binge. ASEAN's corporates now have six times more debt than they did in 1997. Indonesian and Malaysian governments and companies have issued more US dollar debt in 2015 than they did in 2014. This has occurred even as their bond yields were rising and their currencies were weakening.

The unravelling could be driven by three C's—consumers, commodities and currencies. The **consumer sector** has been at the heart of the debt upsurge. Consumer spending, in turn, has spurred corporate investment.

The Thai 7-Eleven operator CP All, controlled by Dhanin Chearavanont is emblematic of debt-fuelled extravagance. CP All's interest coverage ratio has collapsed from six times in 2013 to 1.3 times in 2015. In 2013, CP All agreed to pay US$6 billion for Siam Makro, a listed hardware store. The price tag valued Siam Makro at 45 times estimated earnings for 2013. This exorbitant price was twice the average valuation garnered by retailers in 20 other acquisitions in Asia's emerging markets over the past five years.

Strangely, CP All once had a large stake in Siam Makro but it sold that stake in 2005. The price CP All paid to acquire Siam Makro in 2013 was 13 times what it sold the asset for only eight years before. CP All's net gearing is now 5.7x.

The Siam Makro acquisition was made with fanciful expectations. It was hoped that Thai consumer spending would grow indefinitely. In fact, consumer spending has fallen sharply in the face of political upheaval and weak demand for Thai exports. CP All's same-store growth has averaged just 3% in the last four quarters. It is unlikely to improve, as the company has relentlessly added up to 600 new stores.

The commodity sector has also been a prominent issuer of debt. This region is a major producer of palm oil, copper, and rubber. The decade-long commodity boom enticed ambitious commodity companies to borrow heavily. Wilmar International, the world's biggest palm oil processor, has been particularly aggressive in its capital expenditure. In the last five years, its capital expenditure totalled some $6.6 billion. The company now has US$15 billion of net debt, five times the level in 2010, and mostly denominated in US dollars. Wilmar's market capitalisation is US$13 billion.

The trouble is that a decent return from this intense investment seems to be elusive. There is a glut of palm oil processing capacity. Palm oil processing capacity exceeds palm oil supply by 50% in Indonesia. As with CP All, Wilmar's foot is firmly on the expansion peddle despite the adversity. Wilmar has stated that they would continue with a capex programme of over US$1 billion annually.

Currency exposure is the third factor that may be the region's undoing. The Indonesian rupiah and Malaysian ringgit are at their lowest levels versus the US dollar since 1998. Currency depreciation may spark a bitter end for the debt-fuelled expansion. According to S&P, foreign-currency debts have risen three times more rapidly than local debt for Malaysian, Philippine and Indonesian companies since 2010.

A case in point is Thai Beverage, which took on S$3.6 billion of debt to acquire a nearly 30% stake in Singaporean conglomerate Fraser & Neave. A large portion of the debt is in US dollars while the revenues are in the regional currencies.

The current situation has chilling parallels with 1997. However, a harrowing crisis is unlikely. The region's currency mismatch is not as dire as 18 years ago. Foreign currency borrowing is only 34% of Malaysia's GDP. It was 60% at the end of 1998. Also, non-performing loans are about 10% compared to 50% in 1997.

Nevertheless, a nasty shock from the vile mixture of the three C's may be looming.

Postscript

ASEAN has avoided another 1997 crash, as the piece predicted. The markets have not performed strongly, but a currency crisis has been averted.

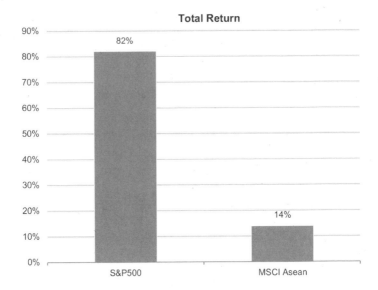

Total Return

Why Jim Rogers is wrong to ditch India

Published on November 4, 2015

Jim Rogers is a feted investor who amassed a fortune alongside George Soros in the 1970s. The Alabama-native said in September that he had turned bearish on India: "I did sell my India shares as I don't see anything happening… there was nothing new coming from Modi," he said at the time. "You can't just invest on hope."

It was a scathing indictment from an investor who craves attention. With his sharp wit and penchant for bow ties, Rogers is a favourite of the financial media. His move to Singapore so that his daughters could learn Mandarin in clean air drew headlines. It was hailed as a wise move by the billionaire investor.

Yet, Rogers is often spectacularly wrong. His bet on a commodity super-cycle seems unfounded. His own Rogers Commodity Index is now 61% below its 2008 peak. In 2012, Rogers proclaimed that the dollar was doomed. Since then, the greenback has appreciated 23% against the euro. Also, with the haze from Indonesia, the air quality in Singapore has been dire lately.

His dismissal of India may be his worst faux pas. Rogers was actually bullish on India last year, when Modi was elected to office. I was, too. For the first time since independence, India had a leader who is an unvarnished supporter of free markets. The fears of China's financial collapse have been so stark, that China's ills are being visited on other emerging markets.

Investors shouldn't allow China to obscure India's awesome potential as a capitalist success. Only 34 years ago, China was poorer than India. Today, China's GDP per capita is five times that of India's. Since Deng Xiaoping's reforms in 1978, growth has averaged 9.8% annually. Since the turn of the millennium, China's GDP has surpassed that of Italy, UK, France, Germany, and Japan. China is now the world's second largest economy. It also has the world's largest foreign reserves, about one-third of the world's total reserves.

India began liberalizing its economy in 1991, but it hasn't grown as fast as China. In fact, it is very unlikely to overtake China now. "If India grows by 8 percent for the rest of this decade and China grows by 7 percent, China will still create another three India's before the decade is over," according to Jim O'Neill, the economist who coined the term BRIC.

However, the link between GDP growth and stock market performance is tenuous. Since December 1992, the MSCI India index has actually outperformed the MSCI China index by 10%. Even after China's stock market went ballistic, MSCI India has exceeded MSCI China by 5.2%. In fact, since the beginning of 1996, the MSCI India index has outpaced the performance in US dollar terms of Berkshire Hathaway, the investment vehicle of billionaire investor Warren Buffett.

Will India's market continue to outperform with Narendra Modi leading the nation? India's leader is a stout man who, in contrast to his predecessor Manmohan Singh, has a limited command of English and economics. He was elected on a pledge to replace red tape with a red carpet for investors. He has vowed to improve infrastructure.

Modi has implemented some of the promised reforms. He has instituted a novel approach to India's massive bad loan burden. India's anachronistic bankruptcy laws means that bad loans linger under the pretence of restructuring. Modi's government wants to convert non-performing loans into equity stakes.

Modi has also streamlined India's cumbersome labour laws. It is difficult to dismiss industrial workers in India. India's employers have always been wary of hiring due to the regulatory burdens. But now, companies can use fixed-term contracts as an efficient alternative to permanent employment. This is a simple step that could create a vast industrial expansion. Other radical steps include cutting the corporate tax from 34% to 25%, which is the level in other emerging markets.

Happily, India is also benefitting from the steep fall in oil prices over the past year. India is chronically dependent on oil imports. The oil price has had a greater impact on its balance payments than foreign portfolio investment. In 2014, India saved US$25 billion on oil imports, which is almost twice the portfolio investment in the country.

Also, India's liberalization has been more comprehensive than China's. China has listed state-owned companies. The management and control is effectively with the Communist Party. In contrast, India has privatized the country without privatizing state companies. It introduced competition in aviation, media and ports, without privatizing the state-owned incumbents. In 1991, India had a single domestic airline – Indian Airlines. Today, Indian Airlines is one of 22 airlines. Capitalism requires competition and not state-owned monopolies like you have in China.

India is a capitalist society that is finally shrugging off a socialist state. Rogers would be disappointed that Singapore's air has been darkened by the haze. He may also rue abandoning India.

Postscript

India has rallied strongly, defying Rogers' pessimism. It has outperformed commodities.

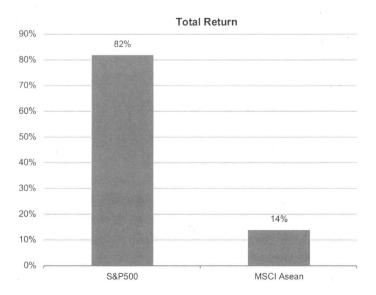

Total Return

S&P500: 82%
MSCI Asean: 14%

Investing in Iran's isolation

Published on August 27, 2015

Last week, I accosted Salman Rushdie in a New York bar. Rushdie is the author of *The Satanic Verses*, which was published in 1988. He spent a decade in hiding after Iran's supreme leader Ayatollah Khomeini called for his assassination for alleged blasphemy. Rushdie adopted the codename Joseph Anton, while he was guarded by the British Secret Service. These days, Rushdie moves around freely. He speaks to random strangers like me with confidence and courtesy.

My chance meeting with the famous writer happened just as Iran is emerging from decades of isolation. Since the US hostage crisis of 1979, Iran has been subjected to onerous sanctions. Investors have been barred from its vast market. This year, the Obama administration reached a nuclear deal with Iran. It paves the way for the Middle Eastern nation to rejoin the global trading system.

Iran has the world's fourth largest proven oil reserves and the second largest natural gas reserves. Yet, the principal attraction of this country of 80 million people may be its consumer and financial sectors rather than its energy resources. Even during its isolation and devastating war with Iraq, its consumer spending flourished.

For instance, in 2012, at the height of the sanctions, Iranians spent US$77 billion on food and $22 billion on clothing. They also spent US$18.5 billion on overseas travel. Today, Iranian consumers still treasure American brands. Tissues are still referred to as Kleenex. Photocopies are known as Xerox. Old-timers fondly recall driving Chevrolets, Buicks and Cadillacs before the 1979 revolution.

Meanwhile, Iran does not have the heavy consumer debt that afflicts ASEAN. MasterCard, Visa and Amex are effectively barred from the country. While Thailand's consumer debt is now 85% of its GDP, Iran has negligible consumer debt. If the sanctions end and foreign banks are allowed to operate in Iran, consumer finance could flourish. This would spur the sales of consumer items ranging from washing machines to cars.

Also, there are five millions Iranians overseas. They are highly credentialed and prosperous with an estimated spending power that matches Iran's GDP of US$370 billon. Their potential return could provide a fillip to consumer spending and investment. The West's embrace of Vietnam in the mid-1980s had a similar catalytic role in its revival.

Iran's authoritarian political structure isn't as backward as some might think. While it is a theocratic state where the mullahs dominate, Iran is the only country in the Middle East that holds Western-style elections, where both men and women can vote. In fact, there are more women in elected office in Iran than in the US, according to *Hedgehogging* by Barton Biggs.

Unlike other countries that are emerging from isolation like Myanmar and Cuba, Iran has a large and liquid stock market. Companies listed on the Tehran Stock Exchange have a combined market capitalization of over US$103 billion, which is about a quarter of the MSCI Frontier Index. Market turnover tops US$100 million a day, which is around the level of the Philippines. On some days, it can trade up to US$400 million.

However, with hardly any foreign investors participating in the market, stock valuations are very low. Iranian stocks are trading at about five times earnings and offer a dividend yield of over 13%.

Of course, Iran's return from isolation is not certain. The current UN sanctions would only be eased if Iran meets certain conditions. The sanctions are also so firmly entrenched that dismantling them could take several years. Even after they are dismantled, foreign banks and multinationals might choose to err on the side of caution for some time.

Still, the prospect of Iran's return to global capitalism is brighter than at any other point since 1979. How can investors get exposure? There are a few ETFs that are investment proxies for Iran. The **iShares MSCI UAE Capped ETF** provides access to 25 stocks in the UAE, which counts Iran as its fourth largest trading partner. Financials are over two-thirds of the ETF's weight. There are also several Middle East ETFs that provide similar exposure. They include the **WisdomTree Middle East Dividend ETF** and the **Market Vectors Gulf State ETF.**

Iran could be capitalism's last untapped frontier. If so, Iran's mullahs will be more interested in courting fund managers than condemning writers like Rushdie.

Postscript

It was hoped that Iran's isolation would end with its nuclear deal. However, the Trump administration reversed the US rapprochement with Iran. The securities that were exposed to Iran's rise have floundered.

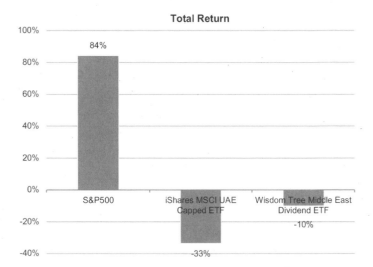

Total Return

S&P500	84%
iShares MSCI UAE Capped ETF	-33%
Wisdom Tree Middle East Dividend ETF	-10%

Learning about the risks and rewards of frontier markets from Burmese Beer

Published on June 23, 2015

Rip Van Winkle is a story about a villager who sleeps for 20 years. After he rises from his slumber, he finds that the world has passed him by.

Myanmar, the Rip Van Winkle of Asia, was an isolated pariah state for decades. From 1962 to 2011, the country was ruled by a military junta that wielded absolute power despite wide condemnation. In 2011, the military junta loosened its grip and the country is now open to investment.

Three years on, the vestiges of Myanmar's long slumber are still plainly evident. Barely two-fifths of the country's 51 million people have a mobile phone. Even consumer goods like soft drinks and instant noodles are in shortage. Its citizens have only just discovered ATMs, credit cards and iPhones over the last three years.

Yet, there is one consumer item that Myanmar's tormented people were not denied even during the country's dark era – beer. In 1995, Fraser & Neave, a Singaporean conglomerate, entered into a joint venture with the Union of Myanmar Economic Holdings (UMEHL), a wing of the Burmese military, to produce beer. Together, they formed **Myanmar Brewery** (MBL), which has a commanding market position in Burma's tiny beer industry.

In 2013, I was part of the flood of curious business visitors who arrived in Myanmar. I sampled MBL's products in Yangon's watering holes. The immense potential of the business became clear to me. F&N's investment in MBL was one of the largest foreign investments in the country. MBL is already the country's largest taxpayer, with revenues of over US$250 million. In FY2014, MBL's earnings rose 50%. But beer consumption in Myanmar is still at a nascent stage.

Vietnam, a country with a similar income and culture to Myanmar, has eight times Myanmar's beer consumption per capita. Myanmar's beer industry seems to be on the same trajectory as that of Vietnam, Cambodia and Sri Lanka when their isolation ended. Vietnam was closed to consumerism until around 1985. Cambodia opened its doors around 1995. Sri Lanka was embroiled in a vicious conflict that ended in 2009. Since then, visitor arrivals has accelerated in these countries and beer sales have boomed.

MBL's success is a shining example of the merits of consumer opportunities in frontier markets. Beer is a cheaper and safer alternative to the crude, homemade hard liquor that is common in these markets. Indeed, beer is viewed as an aspirational intoxicant. Andaman Gold, one of MBL's main brands, has 8% alcohol content.

MBL is also an example of the potent mix of branding, expertise and incumbency. UMEHL has unparalleled logistical capability. Incumbency is a powerful moat in Vietnam and Sri Lanka, too. In Vietnam, for instance, demand for beer has been growing by 15% per annum.

Yet, new entrants have floundered.

MBL's brands such as Myanmar Double Strong and Andaman Gold are ubiquitous and respected in Yangon. The brewing is based on the processes of Asia Pacific Breweries (APB), which F&N once jointly controlled with Heineken. (APB was F&N and Heineken's joint venture vehicle in Asia. But Heineken opted out of investing in MBL because of the sanctions on Myanmar at the time. APB has since been privatised by Heineken).

Recent developments at MBL has highlighted the severe risks that accompany the rewards of frontier markets. UMEHL's principals are connected to the Burmese military. It is projected as a welfare organisation for the officers. In 2014, UMEHL launched a claim on F&N's 55% stake in MBL. The argument was that the change in control of F&N after it was acquired by companies linked to Thai billionaire Charoen Sirivadhanabhakdi meant that UMEHL should have the chance to buy F&N's stake in MBL.

Last November, commercial arbitrators in Singapore ruled in favour of UMEHL. The arbitrators also ruled that an independent valuer will determine the value of F&N's stake in MBL.

The loss of its stake in MBL is a blow to F&N, shaving off a fifth of its value. It also casts a cloud over Thai Beverage, which spent S$3.6 billion on a 29% stake in F&N (before the demerger). Thai Beverage has outperformed the STI by 129% in the last three years, and currently trades at 20 times earnings. F&N trades at 27 times earnings. Those valuations partly reflect the euphoria around the opportunities in Myanmar. The growth in the rest of their businesses is comparatively tepid. For instance, beer volume growth in Thailand is just 4%.

Myanmar may have just risen from its deep sleep, but its thirst for beer is already lucrative. Investors, however, must tread gingerly.

Postscript

Myanmar has shone brightly. Fraser & Neave, a proxy for Myanmar, has outperformed S&P500. Thai Beverage's weakness could be due to exposure to Thailand's pandemic slowdown.

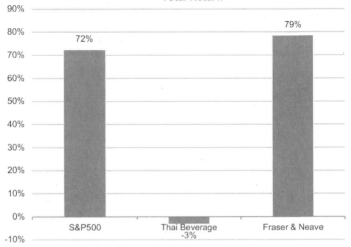

Total Return

S&P500: 72%
Thai Beverage: -3%
Fraser & Neave: 79%

Is the ASEAN conglomerate model losing its shine?

Published on January 10, 2020

Like vinyl records and sideburns, conglomerates in America are a 1970s phenomenon now fast becoming obsolete. In their heyday, conglomerates like International Telephone and Telegraph Corp (ITT) commanded massive stock market premiums.

Investors in Asian conglomerates would be well-placed to heed the lessons of the hero of the golden age of American conglomerates. Harold "Hal" Geneen wasn't just the CEO of ITT from 1959 to 1977 but a symbol for the conglomerate asset class.

Geneen grew ITT from a telegraph equipment producer with US$765 million in sales to a conglomerate with US$17 billion in revenue in 1970. At its peak, ITT's interests included insurance, hotels, and real estate. It controlled one of the largest private landowners in the US as well as the hotel giant Sheraton.

Under Geneen, ITT also became a serial acquirer of businesses. He completed 350 acquisitions and mergers in 80 countries. This was long before such acquisitive scale was easy due to cheap money.

Geneen's mantra was that large, multi-industry companies provide unmatchable efficiencies. These disparate businesses had nothing in common except their parentage. By building scale, the conglomerates could command a lower cost of capital. Also, it could cut costs and apply a uniform culture. Others that followed ITT's formula in the 1960s included Litton Industries and General Electric.

Geneen was a tireless worker who ruled by fear and numbers. He worked the hours of a convenience store – from 7am to 11pm. His *New York Times* obituary said that "he was a man who always needed to know everything".

The ITT senior executives had to send him weekly reports on their targets. They were exceptionally detailed even in the pre-excel era. In a typical month, he read 146 reports with a total of 2,537 pages. All the reports from far-flung managers were sent to him directly, removing the prospect of tampering from middle managers.

But Geneen was not just an outstanding manager. He timed his exit to perfection. By 1977, conglomerates could no longer monopolise efficiencies. Their relative returns started to falter and siloed corporations were more in vogue.

By the mid-1990s – following a series of splits and disposals – the scale of ITT was reduced. It became a mid-size producer of industrial and aerospace parts. Other conglomerates suffered a similar fate. Litton Industries, for example, was acquired by Northrop Grumman in 2001 while General Electric suffered the ignominy of being booted off the Dow Jones Index in 2018 after more than a decade as a component stock there.

ASEAN conglomerates, such as **Jardine Matheson**, **Salim Group** and **San Miguel**, have long enjoyed a relative premium valuation. In 2000-2019, the leading conglomerates in Singapore, Malaysia, Indonesia and the Philippines have traded at an average premium of 21% over the market.

Investors were enamoured by the scale and efficiency that a conglomerate like San Miguel could generate. It operates a vast swathe of businesses from beer to petroleum refining. Its cost of capital, corporate governance and operating efficiency was believed to be superior to its focused rivals. For much of this period, the enthusiasm was warranted, as they have outperformed the market in total shareholder return terms.

The reverence with which the market views ASEAN conglomerates may be about to wane. The Salim Group's constellation of business interests range from mining in the Philippines to noodles in Indonesia. Its CEO Anthoni Salim is known to have a similar work ethic to Geneen, as well as faith in numeracy.

The Hong Kong-listed **First Pacific** is at the pinnacle of the Salim Group's organisational chart with a gross asset value of US$5.7 billion. First Pacific's discount to its sum of the parts (SOTP) valuation has widened from 23% five years ago to 57% today. This indicates a steepening conglomerate discount. In that period, its total shareholder return has plummeted to 9%, well below the TSR for ASEAN pure plays.

From 2014 to 2019, ASEAN conglomerates have delivered a TSR of 10% compared to 13% for pure plays. A study by Bain Consulting Group has also shown that ASEAN conglomerates have underperformed in terms of revenue growth and margins. The conglomerate premium diminishes as an economy prospers. This is especially apparent in the cost of capital. Thailand has tripled its GDP per capita since the Asian Financial Crisis.

Thai pure plays such as **Thai Beverage** raised US$ 2.1 billion in a domestic bond issue in 2018 at just 3%, which is close to an American cost of capital. It is similar to the rate that a Thai conglomerate like **Charoen Pokphand Group,** which has interests ranging from agriculture to retail to telecommunications, could command.

The 2020s may be the decade that ASEAN conglomerates are eroded. Shorting them would be a winning strategy.

Postscript

Shorting the conglomerates has worked out well. Their models seem to be weak in a pandemic.

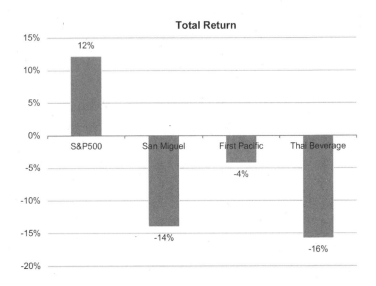

Poor consumers are a big opportunity

Published on September 08, 2015

The rise of the Asian middle class is a clichéd investment theme that almost every strategist has used. The hackneyed rhetoric has obscured the fortune at the bottom of the pyramid in Asia. It is the poor, not the middle classes, that will drive Asia's consumption.

In Indonesia, for instance, the poor represent nearly three-fourths of the country's population of 300 million. The poor, defined as those who earn less than US$4 a day, vastly outnumber the middle classes. Though the average income is around US$10 a day, the overwhelming majority earn less than half that amount.

The Indonesians who are devouring Singaporean property are not representative of that iniquitous land. Actually, the poor contribute about 60% of household spending, which is over US$270 billion. Indonesia's economy is expected to grow at 6% a year. By 2020, the poor will spend more than US$400 billion per year.

There are several ways for companies to target the bottom of the pyramid. One is to sell basic items such as noodles, snacks and shampoo in small unit sizes. Unilever has mastered the sale of shampoo in small sachets. The sachets are priced at 20 US cents per unit, which puts it within the reach of ordinary consumers.

Companies can also target the poor by accepting lower margins for their basic products. They can compensate for this by pricing shampoo for the prosperous customers at a premium. **Unilever Indonesia** sells Lux shampoo in fancy packaging, as well as in simple sachets.

Selling basic items to the poor makes impeccable commercial sense. The sales of noodles, soap and milk are not vulnerable to the economic cycle. By the sharpest of contrasts, middle class consumers can be fickle in their taste for cars and handbags. Indonesia escaped the ravages of the 2008-09 world recession due to the resilient spending by the poor.

A clinching example is the relative sales of cars and motorcycles during the 2008-09 crisis. In that period, car sales collapsed by a fifth in Indonesia. Motorcycles, which are accessible to the poor on a hire purchase basis, fell only 5%.

At a corporate level, the resilience is even more telling. Unilever Indonesia has a vice-like grip on Indonesia's consumer growth, as its product are used by two-thirds of the people. Its market capitalization represents over 2% of Indonesia's GDP. Its reliance on the poor means that it has weathered the 2008-9 crisis, while other emerging market companies suffered. Its annual sales growth has been almost 20% in each of the last eight years.

Companies that sell to the masses such as Unilever have the singular ability to pass on raw material cost hikes. This is particularly relevant, as the rupiah has fallen by 22% in the last year.

The company is expanding, even in the face of a severe economic slowdown in Indonesia. They are spending over US$110 million in the next three years to widen their sales of cheap household items and food.

Other companies are now getting into the act. **Nestlé** has just launched a novel chocolate product in Indonesia – crunch wafers. It was designed with the ordinary consumer as the principal market. The crunch wafers are tiny crispy triangles filled with chocolate. They are sold for 10 US cents a unit.

Home-grown companies are also replicating the success of the multinationals. **Charoen Pokphand Indonesia** sells noodles priced at 20 US cents a pack. They enjoy about 70% market share in the noodle market. Their success has transformed consumer habits. For the first time, it is cheaper to buy a pack of noodles than a bowl of rice. This is a radical change in Indonesia, where rice consumption per capita is one of the highest in the world.

Investors are retreating from emerging markets due to China's slowdown and the commodity collapse. As they rush for the door, they may be forsaking an opportunity to bet on the reliability of poor consumers.

Postscript

Charoen Pokphand Indonesia has shone brightly. Its noodles are popular with the poor. Unilever Indonesia's underperformance could be a consequence of a shift away from MNCs.

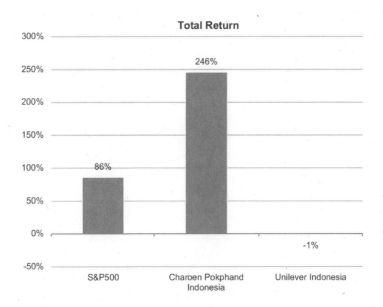

Let us raise a glass to the ThaiBev listing

Published on December 6, 2019

Former US President Franklin D. Roosevelt (FDR) helped win World War II, but his memory will ring long with beer drinkers for another reason. The US had outlawed alcohol from 1920 to 1933. This gave rise to illicit booze, which created an unmanageable crime rate, with gangsters such as Al Capone murdering with impunity. In 1933, FDR ended Prohibition. To wide acclaim.

The end of the Prohibition era brought a novelty to the beer industry: cans. Canning was to the beer industry what sliced bread was to the loaf.

In those days, beer was almost exclusively sold in bottles. Beer lovers feared that the taste of beer from cans would be unpalatable. However, by 1955, most beer sold in the US was in cans. Beer consumption more than doubled from 1933 to 1955.

Southeast Asia is now at a similar juncture as the US was in the 1930s. Most beer in Asia is still sold in bottles. Bottles hamper sales. They break easily and can be difficult to ship.

Bottles are also a weight on cash flow. They belong to the brewer and are more expensive than the beer. Bottles need a refundable deposit. The sale is not consummated until the bottle is returned.

On the other hand, cans are stackable and transportable. The breakage of cans is a lot rarer than bottles. The brewer completes the sales quickly. This is the principal reason that brewers in the West have superior cash flow generation compared to emerging market brewers such as **Thai Beverage** (ThaiBev) and **Saigon Beer Alcohol Beverage** (Sabeco).

Cans are at a nascent stage in ASEAN. Brewers are raising canning capacity. Canned capacity may triple in a decade.

On November 29, the region's largest brewer, Thai Beverage, said that it was looking to list its beer business in Singapore. It is the second-largest brewer in Thailand and controls Saigon Beer (Sabeco), Vietnam's leading brewer.

ThaiBev's beer business could be valued at up to US$10 billion ($13.6 billion), according to media reports. It is possible that the IPO could raise over US$2 billion, which would make it the largest IPO in Singapore since 2000. It would also vastly reduce ThaiBev's US$6.5 billion of net debt.

Asia is the engine room of the world's beer growth. Beer consumption is galloping at more than 6% a year in Vietnam. Vietnam's per capita beer consumption is 43 litres, making it the third highest in Asia after China and Japan.

Vietnam's beer business is mainly a volume growth story, but cans could be a game changer. There is also the prospect of premiumisation once prosperity rises. Vietnam's GDP per capita is a fourth of China's.

Asia's effervescent beer volumes compare favourably with the tepid growth in the West. In Europe and the US, brewers are stagnant.

Although the US and Europe drink about 47% of the world's beer, the figure is shrinking in absolute terms. Germany drinks 109 litres of beer per annum, which is more than twice that of Vietnam.

However, the per capita beer consumption level has shrunk 4% in the last decade.

Beer consumption has dropped by a third in Germany since 1973, despite its being the home of the Oktoberfest beer extravaganza.

Demographics are the dampener in Europe. There are far less youthful rowdies disrupting football matches. Europe is ageing.

In the US, craft brewers are eclipsing conventional brewers. Craft brewers are indecent brewers who frequently sell onsite. Brewerkz on Clarke Quay is a craft brewer. In 2018, craft beer revenue rose 5%, while traditional brewing struggled.

Asia holds the opportunity. Beer consumption in Indonesia is just 1% of the level in Europe. Home brew, the Indonesian version of craft beer, is unrecorded. Indonesia's home brew market could be higher than the official beer market. Once conventional players such as ThaiBev expand in Indonesia, home brew drinkers could trade up.

The IPO could provide ThaiBev with the means to expand. ThaiBev controls the Chang brand, which has potential in the rest of ASEAN.

ThaiBev has returned 273% since its listing in 2006. There may be more fizz as beer cans sweep the region.

Postscript

ThaiBev has suffered due to COVID-19. Its listing of the beer business in Singapore has not materialized.

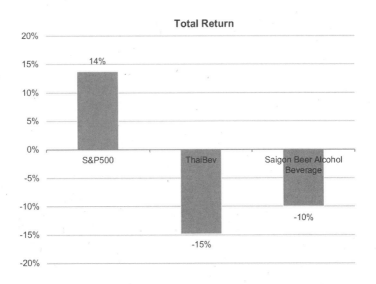

Total Return

INVENTIONS

The cheap washing machine may power the wheels of growth in ASEAN

Published on March 8, 2016

Money laundering is a serious concern for investors. However, laundering of a different kind may be a beacon of light in emerging markets.

Though the washing machine is a common appliance, its exact origins are obscure. As with the iPhone and the electric bulb, its genesis lies in the fertile soil of America. The invention is credited to Alva J. Fisher, who patented the first electric washer in 1908, and was the founder of the Hurley Machine Company in Chicago.

Fisher designed the Thor electric washing machine. The Thor was a drum type washing machine. It had a galvanized tub and an electric motor, which made a tiresome racket.

We do not know whether Fisher wanted his product to be available to the masses. The details of his technical training are sketchy. Fisher's background and motivations are murky, but his impact is crystal clear.

Before the introduction of the electric washing machine, Western women faced drudgery. Washing clothes was cumbersome and labour-intensive. It could take many hours to wash, scrub and dry clothes. Along with cooking and child-rearing, washing was the principal task of a married woman. It was an impediment to women joining the workforce. The mass production of clothing around the turn of the century had created a huge burden of washing. Even with its introduction in 1908, the prospect of instant washing was raised. Though the initial contraptions were unwieldy and expensive, the ball was set in motion. The early washing machines, such as Thor, were like the early mainframe computers. A middle class home could neither afford to buy it or maintain it. Also, they were too heavy to find their way into the pokey homes of urban America.

In just over 30 years after its introduction, the washing machine was found in 40% of the homes in the US. Electricity was almost universal in the American household. The washing machine was the most treasured application of electricity apart from the light bulb. The annual use of electricity in the US went from 79 kilowatt hours per capita in 1902, to 960 kWh per capita in 1929.

In 1940, the main hurdle for the universalisation of the washing machine in the US was affordability. A typical Sears Roebuck washing machine cost US$92 at the time. This was equal to three weeks' wages of a median income person. Washing machines required a huge down payment, which was equal of about 75% of its face value.

Today, washing machines are found in every American home. The contraption is far more elaborate with front loading and attachable dryer. The road to its ubiquity was paved by two innovations–hire purchase and product segmentation.

American retailers such as Macy's and K-Mart created a credit scheme where consumer appliances could be paid for gradually. The down payment would only be just a tenth of its value. The purchaser could pay for it over five years.

Product segmentation meant that the scale of a washing machine could vary. The early units adopted the one-size-fits-all principle. After 1940, smaller and simpler washing machines were sold. These were targeted at the poorer consumers. The cost could range from US$2,500 in today's terms to US$78.

The washing machine may become a mass market product like the TV in poor countries.

The humble washing machine could liberate women in emerging markets from the drudgery of housework. It could unleash a more productive workforce.

There are uncanny parallels between the US in 1940 and the emerging markets of ASEAN. Electricity has spread far and wide in Indonesia, Malaysia, Thailand and Vietnam. However, the washing machine is beyond the means of the poor. The opportunity lies not with the middle classes but at the bottom of the pyramid. In Indonesia, 75% of households have electricity but less than 25% have a washing machine.

The challenge of straddling the pyramid is being mastered by a slew of ambitious Asian companies. These include **Haier** of China and the Korean duo of **LG** and **Samsung**.

Haier has proved particularly adept at market segmentation. It produces sturdy and cheap washing machines for rural users. The old models typically get clogged with mud. Cultivators were using them to clean vegetables, apart from clothes. A washing machine can now cost about 10 days' wage of a median income person in Indonesia. Haier also makes fancy washing machines for urban dwellers, who live in small flats.

The rhetoric about the rise of the ASEAN middle classes is tired and misleading. Investors in this region should take companies that target the poor more seriously. Their dirty laundry may provide a compelling investment opportunity, as well as cleanse their stock portfolios.

Why food delivery stocks
are steaming hot

Published on August 14, 2020

Tony Jannus was an American pilot who flew the world's first commercial airline flight. It was between St Petersburg and Tampa in the US state of Florida in 1914. He instantly became a celebrity. Pilots were then feted like astronauts. The dashing Jannus had a vast female following.

But his name will ring long for creating a destructive industry. Commercial flight environmental damage is alarming. Its capital destruction is even worse. In the last 106 years, the airline industry has never made money. COVID-19 may wipe out the airline industry. According to the International Air Transport Association (IATA), the aviation industry will lose US$84 billion ($115.4 trillion) this year.

In a strange twist, food delivery is taking off when aviation is collapsing. COVID-19 is wiping out one loss-making industry and boosting another. Food delivery through apps such as Uber Eats, Deliveroo and Just Eats has risen 71% in 1H2020. In Singapore, Foodpanda and GrabFood have done more business in 1H2020 than in the whole of 2019. Food delivery apps were also the most downloaded in Singapore during the "circuit breaker" period.

Pizza Hut pioneered online food delivery in 1995, when the internet was a curiosity. It has been only in the last five years that it has emerged as a serious industry. The smartphone has fuelled the trend. The total industry is expected to reach US$136 billion this year, which is double the level in 2015. It has reshaped dining habits and disrupted restaurants. The users of online food delivery services have also risen from 1.3 billion in 2014 to over 2.1 billion this year.

There are a raft of listed giants in the field. They are mainly in China and the West. The big gorilla is Chinese shopping platform **Meituan-Dianping**, which has a market capitalisation of US$177 billion. Meituan's sales have risen 10-fold in the last five years. It provides 25 million meals a day, which is more than the total amount of meals provided by the rest of the industry.

Meituan has recently turned a profit, but a sea of red stalks the industry. Other players such as GrubHub and DoorDash in the US and Just Eat in Europe lose about US$0.25 for every dollar of revenue.

This week, Uber reported its results. Uber Eats, its food delivery arm, saw revenues double to US$1.8 billion. Its adjusted EBITDA losses were US$232 million. Despite incredibly fortunate circumstances, it still lost money!

Food delivery has a basic problem. It is a tech business without the network effect. The business is high-tech with a low-tech last mile problem. The average order takes around 30 minutes to execute. A delivery person can, at best, do two deliveries per hour. The more business one undertakes, the more delivery fees accrue to the driver.

The other issue is the crippling operating expenses. The food delivery players have to invest heavily in online marketing. Fave—a popular app in Singapore—provides a $10 discount for any new user. Operating expenses have averaged over 90% for Grubhub in the past three years.

The severe cash burn in this industry will not hinder its growth. Interest rates are so low that hungry investors are eager to fund the cash burn. Amazon took seven years to deliver profits. Many airlines never generated profits, if one accounted for their cost of capital.

The food delivery companies are valued at a multiple of their sales, as they do not even have operating profits. The industry average for the global players is about five times FY2021 EV/Sales. Meituan is the outlier at nine times FY2021 EV/Sales. That may be warranted due to its scale economics in China. It has increased the number of meals served a day by a factor of 10 in five years. There is still room for growth, as only a third of the country is covered.

The major players may scour the world for acquisition targets. The emerging markets of Indonesia, India and Brazil have the ingredients to repeat Meituan's success.

Jannus died in a plane crash in Russia, just two years after his famous flight. He was just 27. Commercial aviation has thrived for the last 104 years, despite its poor returns.

It is still early days for food delivery, as it is only a quarter century old. Companies may crash, but the industry's valuation will soar.

Postscript

Despite the cash burn, food delivery stocks are up. Meituan Dianping, the Chinese giant, could become the Alibaba of food delivery.

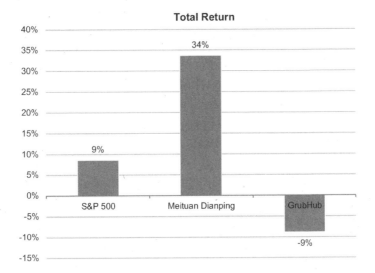

Total Return

Why barbershops are defying death

Published on February 28, 2020

Many years ago, my career coach argued that barber salons were recession-proof. People would need a haircut, whatever the gyrations of the economy. I ignored this advice and became an equity analyst.

Barber salons are not only recession-proof, they are defying the death of traditional retail. Singapore's shrinking footfall in the malls has been accelerated by the coronavirus. But, barber salons are thriving in Singapore and elsewhere.

In the US, barbershops are licensed businesses. This allows us to track its progress. The number of barbershops fell by 23% from 1992 to 2012. Since 2013, there has been a boom. In the last two years, barbershops have risen at about 10% per annum, according to Barber Boards Association of America.

This stands in complete contrast to the crumbling performance of traditional retail. Vanishing footfall is common not just in Singapore. In the US, over 15,000 store locations have closed since 2017. Sales are moving online.

Even businesses that were said to be immune to e-commerce such as cosmetics have fallen victim to it. Cosmetics buyers, it was said, prefer to touch and feel the merchandise. However, more than a quarter of the cosmetics sales in the US in 2019 were online.

What is the secret sauce that gives barbershops its Teflon-like status? A robot cannot provide a reliable and affordable haircut—yet.

We have computer programs that assess the contours of a person's head and hair. But, everyone's hair is sufficiently distinct that only a human can truly assess it. People do not have enough confidence in a machine to allow robotic scissors to cut hair. There is also the fear of injury.

Barber salons, particularly those that cater to males, enjoy regular revenue. Most males have a haircut every month. The same barber has been chopping my thinning locks for the last 22 years. A haircut is a regular function like brushing teeth or shaving.

The male haircut is also a uniform service with high volumes. The ingredients are just a pair of scissors, clippers, a brush, a sink and a chair. In Singapore, there is a service that provides a 10-minute haircut for $10. This is the fast food equivalent of a haircut.

Women's hairdressing is not as uniform and requires higher upfront costs. The women's hair salon carries a vast stock of dyes and cosmetics. Blow-drying adds to the overheads. The efficiency is less, as a hair appointment can take three hours. The frequency is also lower than a male barber shop.

A barbershop is cash flow positive, unlike many other service businesses. The customer pays on delivery of the service. The wages, rent and utility bills are paid at the end of the month.

Landlords love barber shops. Barbershops want a space format that many other tenants avoid. Barber shops want "bowling alley" space—minimal storefront with great depth.

Though most barbershops are standalone, there are stock market proxies. **QB Net Holdings**, listed in Japan, is an operator of budget haircuts in Asia. It has a network of 660 stores in Japan, Taiwan and Singapore. The typical haircut in Japan takes an hour and costs about US$60 ($84).

QB Net provides haircuts in 10 minutes that cost below US$20. Reservations are not required. It targets the 20- to 45-year-old demographic that are looking for quick service. It takes up an average space of around 33sqm.

At just 12 times EV/EBITDA, QB Net is undervalued for its growth. It generated 19% earnings growth in FY2019 and could exceed that in FY2020. Its projected same store sales growth (a vital metric in retail) is twice that of the average in Japan. It is much higher than the moribund norm in Singapore.

Some barber salons may have to take a haircut on the level of service. Supercuts, the UK business of US-listed barber shop operator **Regis Corp**, filed for bankruptcy last year. Supercuts has 220 salons, but struggled due to its extravagant rents and workforce.

The QB Net low-cost and efficient model seems to be the one that will last. It may be too late for me to follow my career coach's advice, but investors should not ignore this business.

Postscript

This piece was written before the pandemic struck. The case for barber shops has actually strengthened. It was one of main retail activities that people craved during the lockdown. Barbershops have shown strong sales. The stocks have performed badly, as part of the retail selldown. This is unfair.

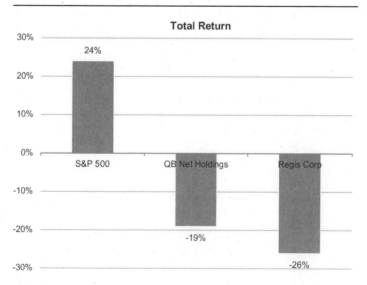

Will the iris herald the biometric revolution?

Published on July 3, 2020

The publishers of The Edge are housed in a simple building on Cecil Street. I last visited *The Edge Singapore* shortly before COVID-19. I was shocked that the method of identification at the lobby had not changed for decades.

Visitors had to write their names and identity card (IC) numbers in an old-fashioned ledger. The IC is then surrendered to the security guard. It is only returned when the visitor leaves the building. There are many risks to the building and the visitor with this system. The IC is accepted at face value. There is a risk to the visitor as the IC is not with him. For example, I forgot to collect my IC, after leaving the building. COVID-19 has also highlighted the risk of infection from physical contact.

This type of identification was still common in many buildings in Singapore until a few weeks ago. COVID-19 has claimed many casualties. It is amazing that this system survived in a city-state that has pioneered biometrics. Biometrics are a person's physical characteristics. Facial recognition like the technology that is used on iPhones is an example. Fingerprints and irises are another form of it.

Many readers may have hazy recollections of airports. Changi Airport was one of the first to use biometric identification for the boarding process. Other countries have followed suit. British Airways estimated that the use of biometrics has halved the time required to board 400 passengers in Los Angeles to 22 minutes.

Biometrics are widely used by banks to identify customers. It is a common standard for PCs. The principal attraction is that it does not require one to verify identity through an object like an IC. One does not have to even remember a password.

However, biometrics are not free of risks. Recently, my wife indulged my identical twin sons with the latest iPad. The twins are almost indistinguishable to the human eye. Even close friends sometimes struggle to tell them apart. They have the same DNA. The iPad can be opened through facial recognition. The younger of the twins opened the other's iPad. Apart from the fraternal tension that this caused, it struck me that facial recognition biometrics have problems.

There is a fool-proof alternative to this issue — iris recognition. The iris is the ring-shaped membrane behind the cornea of the eye. My twins may have the same appearance and genetic makeup, but their iris is unique. In fact, each eye in every person is different. The secret solution to biometrics may indeed be the iris.

But, there is a larger problem with biometrics. What if someone gets hold of the biometric database? If someone loses an IC, it can be invalidated and replaced. A forgotten password can be reset. Biometric data cannot be replaced or reset.

This danger came to light when I visited Hong Kong in 2015. An online magazine ran a media campaign to deter people from littering. It had reconstructed people's likeness (not their actual photos) from plastic cans and cigarettes that people had disposed of. A database then reconstructed people's photos from the biometric data in the litter. They had enough clues to recreate the eye colour, skin tone and facial features.

The dangers of stolen biometric data are limitless. We could face a pandemic of stolen identities. Singapore-based company **Infinity Optics**, for example, has even patented iris recognition technology. It is so discerning that it was able to distinguish my twins!

Its secret sauce is that it has also solved the privacy problem. An independent test shows that Infinity Optics technology does not leave a trace of its biometric information in the outcoming codes. This, according to its CEO Alfred Chan, eliminates privacy security risks. If so, Infinity Optics may be going places.

The stock market proxies for biometrics are rare. **BIO-key** is a NASDAQ-listed company that provides fingerprint identification services. **Intellicheck**, listed on NYSE, is a fascinating company that authenticates driving licenses through biometrics. **Datasonic** on the KLSE provides biometrics for the Malaysian government. All three of these stocks have doubled since March, beneficiaries of the COVID-19 hysteria.

The market for this technology is massive. As investors come to grips with its potential, they should welcome the end of the ledger books.

Postscript

Intellicheck has risen sharply as Biometrics increases its allure. The pandemic has accelerated the attention on the sector.

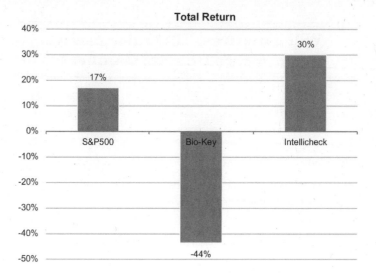

Total Return

- S&P500: 17%
- Bio-Key: -44%
- Intellicheck: 30%

Will a mattress IPO raise Asian e-commerce from its slumber?

Published on January 31, 2020

The sleepy US IPO market could be woken up by an online mattress company. Casper, a pioneer in online mattress sales, is the first major IPO in 2020.

Mattresses were resistant to online sales for many years. People wanted to touch, feel and lie on a mattress before they buy it. A mattress is a delayed and considered purchase, unlike buying groceries online. People buy just three or four mattresses in their lives. A typical customer buys a mattress once every decade.

But there are some features of mattresses that make it a prime candidate for online disruption. It is an opaque industry with comfortable margins. Mattresses consist mainly of foam and can sell for US$1,000 ($1,349).

Mattress stores do not need to hold large inventory. They act as showrooms where customers try out the merchandise.

Comparisons between one company's mattresses are almost impossible, as branding is not uniform. Prices diverge sharply even in the US.

But Casper has shaken up the mattress business. The company was founded in 2014 by Philip Krim, a 36-year-old who first sold mattresses when in university. Online sales of mattresses were rare six years ago.

The company could reach US$400 million in sales this year. These days, more than a sixth of American mattresses are now sold online.

Casper's struggles are a revealing prism with which to

view the march of e-commerce in ASEAN. E-commerce pioneers such as Lazada and Shoppee, subsidiaries of **Alibaba Group Holding** and **Sea** espectively, are facing similar issues. There is a strange symmetry between the proportion of online sales in the ASEAN retail market and the US mattress industry. In 2014, online sales in parts of ASEAN were just 5%.

The ratio has risen sharply since then in both cases.

There are three lessons for ASEAN e-commerce from Casper.

First, the reliability of delivery can make or break an online business.

Casper delivers mattresses in boxes to customer doorsteps. Customers can even receive a box with an inflatable mattress. It takes away the awkwardness of mattress delivery through narrow doorways.

Similarly, Shopee's customers are receiving household goods reliably in fancy packaging. A quarter of the platform's customers also receive free shipping while shipping is also heavily subsidised for the remaining customers. This is a necessary novelty in the ASEAN region, where e-commerce barely existed five years ago.

Casper has a return policy of 100 days. One-fifth of the mattresses are returned. Delivering a 90-pound mattress to a customer and then collecting it is a pain.

Shopee has also grappled with the last mile issue. It operates within ASEAN, a sprawling and diverse region. Indonesia, one of its main markets, has 17,508 islands and three time zones. Shopee reported that a large portion of its gross merchandise value (GMV) in 2018 either failed to deliver or was returned.

Second, aggressive marketing is vital. Casper has aggressively projected its brand, with much of the spending on search advertising and social media. It has spent US$423 million on marketing since the start of 2016, which is almost half its valuation.

At a third of revenue, operating expenses is the main cause of Casper's cash burn. Emerging market players such as Shopee prefer billboards and print ads. However, Shopee's operating expenses have fallen to 4% of revenue in 3Q19 from 10% in 3Q17.

Third, cash flow generation needs to guide valuations. Casper is bleeding cash but it may not bleed to death. Its cash flow from operations (CFO) has shrunk from US$84 million in FY17 to US$30 million in 9MFY19. In contrast, Shopee's EBITDA losses (Sea's e-commerce segment) are mounting, which suggests that it may eventually deplete its parent's cash.

Loss-making e-commerce companies like valuations based on price/sales (P/S) multiples. As many of them are not generating cash, P/S is one of the few metrics. Casper is demanding a P/S multiple of three times, which would give it a market cap of US$1 billion.

Sea is trading at nearly 10 times P/S for FY2020, while the emerging market e-commerce average is 5.4 times. If Casper is looking for just 3 times P/S, Sea seems richly valued. Sea's cash generation is far worse than its sleepy US counterpart.

Casper's customers may sleep soundly on their mattresses. However, the investors in the cash-burning emerging market e-commerce companies may not.

Postscript

Casper's stock price has gone into slumber due to COVID-19. Though e-commerce has benefited from the lockdown, people have avoided replacing their mattresses. Mattresses are expensive purchases that people may postpone during a crisis.

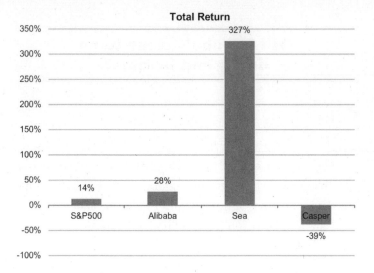

Total Return

Will Alibaba's Hong Kong listing end in tears?

Published on December 6, 2019

Farmers have prospered by making hay while the sun shines. Alibaba Group Holding, the e-commerce giant, is following suit. Its Hong Kong listing on Nov 19 is impeccably timed. It is raising US$13 billion ($17.7 billion) to fund its expansion.

There has been a stampede for the issue, despite the US-China trade war and the crisis in Hong Kong. Media reports suggest that the book is already covered multiple times.

Alibaba is in the pink of health. It recently broke records during Singles Day—the world's largest 24-hour shopping event.

The annual event takes place on November 11 and celebrates the virtues of singlehood in a culture in which the youth face parental pressure to marry. Gross merchandise value (GMV) on Singles Day easily exceeded last year's record of US$30.5 billion.

In 2QFY2020 ended September 30, income from operations was RMB20,364 million ($3,942 million), an increase of 51% y-o-y; adjusted earnings before interest, taxes, depreciation and amortisation rose 39% y-o-y to RMB37,101 million. Net income attributable to ordinary shareholders was RMB72,540 million, and net income was RMB70,748 million, which included a significant one-time gain recognised upon the receipt of the 33% equity interest in Ant Financial. Excluding this one-time gain of RMB69.2 billion and certain other items, non-GAAP net income was RMB32,750 million, an increase of 40% y-o-y.

The listing offers mainland investors a chance to invest in Hong Kong. The Stock Connect programme facilitates mainland investment in the Hong Kong market.

Previously, only Chinese with money parked outside the country could trade the country's most valuable company.

The Hong Kong protests have not dented the pipe that connects Hong Kong to the mainland. US$18 billion has flowed into Hong Kong since the protests began.

Alibaba has been resilient in the face of intense competition from **Tencent Holdings**, **Meituan Dianping** and **Baidu**. The proceeds from this issue would be used to consolidate Alibaba's expansion in cloud computing, entertainment as well as investment in start-ups.

The US-listed Alibaba is up 34% so far this year, which explains the management's rush to the market.

But, there are non-financial reasons for the listing. For one, it is an act of solidarity with Beijing. The Chinese authorities are facing persistent protests in Hong Kong. Listing one of the largest Chinese companies in Hong Kong would cement the city state's position as a leading financial centre.

Also, the trade war looms large on Chinese e-commerce. The US may close the door on Chinese companies. There could be restrictions on Chinese companies that operate in the US as well as accessing the capital markets.

In September, Bloomberg reported that Larry Kudlow, head of President Donald Trump's National Economic Council (NEC), was considering restrictions on Chinese companies that used US financial markets. By listing in Hong Kong, Alibaba insulates itself from the risk of those extreme measures.

The move is spearheaded by the new man at the helm — Daniel Zhang, an uncharismatic accountant. Unlike his heralded predecessor Jack Ma, Zhang rarely pontificates on the secrets of success. He does share Ma's opportunism, as the timing of the listing shows.

However, there is an eerie anniversary that may haunt Alibaba. Alibaba is listing in Hong Kong as the 20th anniversary of the dotcom collapse looms. March 11, 2020 will mark 20 years since the violent convulsions that destroyed US$1 trillion (about 20%) of value on the NASDAQ in a month.

Tech listings used to routinely double on the first day in the late 1990s. NASDAQ was a wonderland where ideas could fetch instant fortunes.

Tiny startups such as Webvan and Pets.com had vast ambitions and valuations, but negligible revenues. These early e-commerce firms were burning their IPO proceeds in a year.

The brutal crash of 2000 exposed the fragilities of the sector. Today, the danger is that the risks are magnified. The current bubble is not with the listed e-commerce players. It is with the huge investments that startups are receiving from other e-commerce players, VCs and angel investors.

The startups have unsustainable cash flows. Once this unpleasant fact becomes apparent, investors such as Alibaba will be stuck with illiquid investments.

Also, this year has seen many mega IPOs of cash flow-negative businesses. Uber raised US$8 billion, while its smaller competitor Lyft raised US$2.3 billion. These businesses promise to disrupt commerce, but they have universally lost money since listing. The market seems to be tiring of unprofitable, cash flow-negative companies, as the WeWork collapse shows.

Already, the Chinese slowdown is affecting Alibaba's competitors. Tencent has reported a 13% drop in earnings in its latest quarter, as a result of weaker advertising and gaming revenue. Alibaba must be heralded for its opportunistic listing but for investors, the party could end in tears.

Postscript
Alibaba and the e-commerce stocks have defied pessimism. The pandemic has provided a massive boost. Their risks remain undiminished.

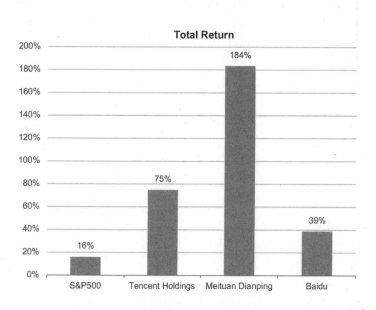

Space may be the final investment frontier

Published on January 3, 2017

John Glenn, the first American to orbit the earth, died at the age of 95 on Dec 8. The definitive event of his life happened before most Americans were born. In February 1962, he circled the planet three times in just under five hours. Glenn returned safely to the adulation of an American public that was eager for their country to match the Soviet Union. Their Cold War adversary had stolen a march over them by sending a man into space a year earlier. Glenn's voyage was a shot in the arm for America's ambitions.

Glenn was feted to the heavens. This austere man from the rural Midwest was given a ticker tape parade. He addressed both houses of Congress, where he received standing ovations. The adulation was unprecedented. It was said (half) jokingly that he could have abolished the constitution and declared himself president.

Glenn may have seen three sunrises during his famous flight, but 54 years later, the sun has yet to rise on space exploration. Intergalactic travel was supposed to be the norm by the 21st century. Humans would speed across the galaxy and settle on planets, as in science fiction serial *Star Wars*.

Planet hopping continues to be the stuff of science fiction, though. The end of the Cold War cut short the rivalry between the US and the Soviet Union. In both countries, space exploration had been subsidised by heavy military spending. Both their space programmes started around the same time and were linked to their military budgets. The fall of the Soviet Union in 1991 resulted in military cutbacks, which curtailed spending on space missions.

Also, a tragedy dampened the American government's appetite and the public's empathy for space. The space shuttle was supposed to be an efficient alternative manned spacecraft. Sadly, this new technology was discredited by the Challenger tragedy in 1986. The shuttle crashed 73 seconds into its flight, killing its seven crew members, one of whom was a schoolteacher. This instantly led to revulsion at the space programme. Space research spending nosedived in the following decade.

Today, the allure of space exploration has been rekindled by a tech billionaire. Elon Musk, a 45-year-old Canadian American, helped found **PayPal Holdings**. This gifted engineer made a fortune pioneering online payments solutions.

He has now set his sights on colonising Mars. Musk founded Space Exploration Technologies (SpaceX), a company that could take a crew of 100 to Mars in the next decade. The cost of the interplanetary trip could be about US$100,000 ($142,350) for each individual. This is about a sixth of the cost of an average HDB flat in Singapore and may make the trip attractive to some. The trips would range in length from 80 to 140 days. SpaceX plans to make the first uncrewed Mars mission in 2018.

The company has spent over US$3 billion on its programme, particularly developing rockets. SpaceX is part of an explosion of investment in space over the last five years. As it is unlisted, there is little visibility on its prospects.

However, there are listed competitors that supply to the space industry. They have profitable core businesses that are not dependent on the volatility of space travel. Their sales are driven by the growing satellite and aerospace industry. Their order books are stable despite the threat of lift-off failures among the likes of SpaceX.

The most prominent of these companies is **Orbital ATK.** The company, which makes rockets and satellites, is about to reap the synergy gains from its recent merger. Its Antares rocket will supply Space-X's International Space Station. Bloomberg consensus expects earnings growth of over 10% in the next three years. But, if SpaceX's Mars mission occurs in 2018, the stock could skyrocket (pun intended).

Lockheed Martin is another proxy for the space race. The giant contractor is developing rockets that are apparently cheaper than SpaceX's. Its valuation is now at a five-year low. John Glenn was a pioneer, but his legacy is incomplete. Investors now have a chance to reap the rewards of his bravery after his death.

Postscript

Lockheed Martin has shone brightly during the space boom. SpaceX has launched rockets and may seek an astronomical valuation in an IPO.

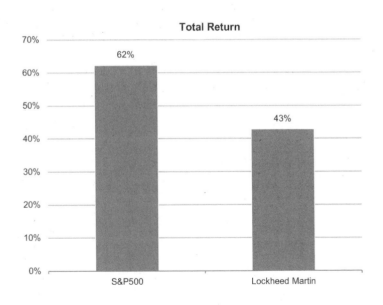

What the Chettiar era tells us about fintech

Published on November 21, 2016

Singapore is a financial centre with gleaming towers full of banks. The world's leading banks adorn the skyline. The bankers are cosmopolitan and hail from Greenland to New Zealand.

But up to the early 1960s, Singapore's banking was dominated by a South Indian community called the Chettiars. The Chettiars are a caste of merchants who enjoyed exclusive status as financial intermediaries in many parts of the British empire, such as Burma, Ceylon and British Malaya (which then included Singapore). They acted for the big British banks such as Standard Chartered and The Hong Kong and Shanghai Bank (now HSBC).

In Singapore, the big British banks lent to the Chettiars, who would in turn lend to local borrowers. The Chettiars were liable for the loans and collected an interest spread in return. As agents of the banks, the Chettiars had to understand the financial standing of their borrowers. On the other hand, the banks were able to maintain a lean staff. In modern financial parlance, the Chettiars were loan underwriters for the banks and disintermediated their risk.

The Chettiar moneylenders congregated near the banks of the Singapore River, along Market Street and Chulia Street. Their tiny living quarters and offices were called *kittingis*. Besides financing, the Chettiars were also able to organise international fund transfers and provided safekeeping services.

They thrived for several decades. But things changed. In the 1930s, there was a slump in commodity prices and a major economic depression. In the 1940s, the Japanese occupied Singapore. After the war, finance became more tightly regulated.

In 1951, the Moneylenders Act was introduced, which severely restricted the activities of the Chettiars. Many closed their businesses, and their influence waned.

In the past few years, a new breed of financial intermediaries has arisen. Using technology, they are disintermediating the role of banks in different ways. Crowdfunding platforms are matching providers of funds with borrowers. It is now possible to make payments via smartphones. Blockchain could soon revolutionise trade financing and loosen the hold that banks have over it.

Fintech investment in Asia has risen 40-fold since 2010 to US$4.3 billion ($5.9 billion) in 2015. Singapore is at the forefront of the trend. With a solid infrastructure and being relatively wealthy, it is an ideal testing ground for new technologies. The government has also thrown its weight behind it. The Monetary Authority of Singapore is planning to spend US$225 million in the next five years to support fintech innovation.

The cutting edge of fintech is not the banks, though. Instead, it is the startup companies that have introduced new ideas like peer-to-peer lending. P2P lending involves lending money through online platforms that match lenders and borrowers.

It eliminates intermediaries such as banks and their agents. P2P started in 2005 with a British company called Zopa and has since spread widely in developed markets.

P2P lenders are effectively modern-day Chettiars, providing funds to borrowers more quickly and efficiently than banks. P2P is particularly appealing to the masses in Asia, who do not have ready access to credit. Over two-thirds of people in ASEAN countries do not have a credit card because the traditional banks have excluded them.

MoolahSense is among the P2P lenders in Singapore. Founded in 2013, it connects local SMEs with investors. Crowdo is another such company. It is a P2P lender in the region with over 20,000 members. **Crowdo** provides crowdfunding for businesses, bypassing banks.

Where will all this lead to? The fintechs of today are making finance cheaper and more efficient. But they aren't immune to the booms and busts that have driven financial markets for centuries. When the availability of funding suddenly expands, the risk of a crushing financial bust is imminent. This immutable principle led to financial calamities such as the Great Depression in the 1930s and the Global Financial Crisis of 2008.

Already, the US-based P2P firm Lending Club, which went public in 2014, is facing defaults. P2P lenders do not earn interest or hold deposits, but they do have to constantly increase their transactions to register profits. The fluctuations of finance apply in the brave new world of fintech, as they did for the Chettiars.

Postscript

Fintech's stock market performance has not matched its promise. Lending Club has collapsed on the weight of its poor delivery.

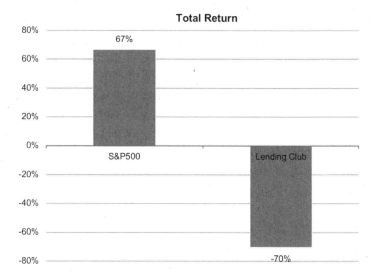

Moleskine proves the enduring value of writing in style

Published on October 24, 2016

The new iPhone 7 has generated a frenzy among devotees of Apple products. Many eagerly waited in line overnight in front of **Apple** stores to get their hands on it. Expert commentators wildly speculated about the device's new features.

Investors have been much less excited, though. Sales of iPhones, which account for more than half of Apple's revenue, have fallen 25% over the last year. This year, Apple's net income is set to decline 15%. As for the new iPhone 7, nearly three weeks after its release, it has achieved an adoption rate of only 2.1%. The iPhone 6 achieved an adoption rate of 4.9% within the same time.

By the sharpest of contrasts, the iPhone 7's tepid reception is unfolding just as a private-equity investor is reaping a big return from an investment in an old-technology product — paper notebooks. Moleskine is a maker of designer notebooks and is listed in Italy. Its success proves that there is big money in a simple notebook despite the digital age.

Syntegra Capital took a majority stake in Moleskine in 2006 for €17 million. The company was then delisted. It relisted in 2013.

This month, Syntegra is exiting the investment for €323 million ($497 million), which is a return of 19 times. D'Ieteren, a Belgian family concern, announced that it will buy Moleskine and delist it from the Milan Stock Exchange.

Moleskine notebooks have a cult following. I am a fan. I have accumulated over 50 of the notebooks in the last decade. They are lined up in chronological order on my bookshelf. They provide me with a tactile feel of the past. In meetings, they allow me to scribble notes without the distraction of beeping messages. The other party receives my complete attention.

Unlike iPhones, Moleskine notebooks never run out of power. They do not require upgrades nor a hefty roaming fee when you cross the border.

The notebooks are bound in cardboard and fastened by an elastic band. The design was perfected by a Parisian bookbinder in the late 1800s. In those days, Paris was the haunt of artists such as Oscar Wilde, Pablo Picasso and Ernest Hemingway. These expatriates discovered the virtues of Moleskine notebooks and spread the word with their fame.

Moleskine's operating margins have averaged 32% in the last three years. This is almost twice the average for luxury brands such as **Tumi Holdings**, **L'Occitane International** and **Prada**. The paper products line makes up more than 90% of Moleskine's revenue. Paper is cheaper than the raw material for luxury wares such as handbags, so Moleskine has greater leeway to mark up the price.

For instance, its standard black notebook sells for $36 in Singapore. A similar but inferior brand of notebook sells for a fifth of that amount at any stationer. Moleskine is not the only producer of premium writing equipment that is thriving in the digital age. It was thought that pencils would become obsolete. However, pencil sales have never been better. Nearly 20 billion pencils are produced each year and more than 50% of them are produced in China.

The emperor in the pencil pack is another venerable company — **Faber-Castell**. The firm was founded in 1761 near Nuremberg in Germany. Over the last 255 years, it has been constantly improving the simple pencil. Its innovations include introducing the hexagonal pencil and placing an eraser on one end.

Faber-Castell's pencils are sturdy, durable and cheap. It produces 2.2 billion pencils annually and is the most profitable stationer in the world. The pencils are particularly popular in poor countries, where eager children are often the first generation to be educated. The firm thrives in the West by producing higher-quality pencils.

India, which has more schoolchildren than any other country, is a fertile ground for producers of pen and paper. There are five listed stationers that are generating earnings growth of more than 15%. **Navneet Education**, the largest among them, has spread its tentacles across the vast country.

Recently, BlackBerry announced that it would stop making its trademark product. At its peak in 2008, the BlackBerry was the handset of choice for professionals. Now, iPhones have made them look anachronistic.

The iPhone may be the leading smartphone today, but as the demise of the **BlackBerry** shows, consumers and technology can be fickle. Its end could be nasty, brutish and short.

Moleskine, Faber-Castell and the Indian stationers will outlast the next generation of smartphones. Investors should not forsake the tried and tested.

Postscript

Apple's Iphones have commanded investor and customer attention. Printed stationers like Navneet Education have not matched it. But, it would be premature to dismiss paper.

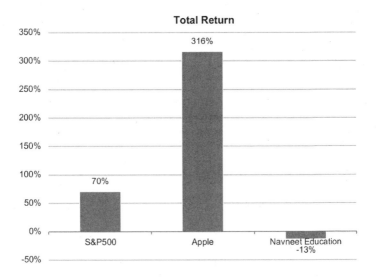

Total Return

- S&P500: 70%
- Apple: 316%
- Navneet Education: -13%

Will dual-class shares bring SGX an F1 listing?

Published on October 10, 2016

Weekend at Bernie's is a 1989 cult movie about two insurance company employees who find their boss Bernie dead. As they wish to enjoy Bernie's luxurious holiday home without arousing suspicion, they prop up Bernie's corpse to pretend that he is alive.

This month, Singapore hosted a different kind of weekend at Bernie's. Nearly 300,000 people lined the streets to watch the annual Formula 1 extravaganza. The world's glitterati descended on the city state for the weekend. There was a string of glitzy events, where champagne flowed and revellers danced into the humid night.

The godfather behind the circus is Bernie Ecclestone, an 85-year-old billionaire who exerts a vice-like grip on the sport. Ecclestone's Herculean drive belies his 5ft 3in frame.

Ecclestone, the son of a fisherman, made his first fortune in the 1960s—long before the current F1 drivers were born. He traded motorcycles and sports cars in London.

Ecclestone soon realised that there were greater rewards from his passion for motor sport. His own foray into racing had ended with a nasty crash in the late 1960s. In 1972, Ecclestone bought a racing team, which gave him membership to the Formula One Constructors' Association (FOCA), which then arranged F1 races.

F1 racing then was a far cry from today's gilded event. It was amateurish and dangerous. The events attracted itinerant businessmen, minor nobility and hangers-on. The fatality rate for the drivers was high.

TV coverage was sporadic. National TV networks occasionally broadcast it. In any case, the set-up made for poor TV viewing. The tracks were muddy and chaotic.

Ecclestone sensed an opportunity to professionalise the sport. The other team-owners had little commercial ability. They were just engineers and retired drivers. He persuaded FOCA to entrust the organisation of the events to him. By 1975, he had become president of FOCA.

This proved to be a masterstroke. It gave Ecclestone the licence to negotiate with race organisers all over the world. The complex logistics of holding the race was handled entirely by him.

For 41 years, Ecclestone has dominated the rewards from the sport. The latest iteration of Ecclestone's control of the game's finances took place 16 years ago. The games governing body is called Federation Internationale de l'Automobile. In 2000, FIA granted Ecclestone the exclusive commercial rights to the F1 until 2110.

The payment for the 110-year deal was US$360 million, the bulk of which would be deferred for decades. Ecclestone has the sole rights to negotiate and collect fees from hosts. Singapore, for instance, had to strike a deal with Ecclestone to hold the races. Ecclestone's exclusivity extends to the TV rights to the 21 races with a six-billion TV audience.

In 1999, private-equity investors took a 50% stake in his holding company. CVC Partners eventually bought a stake with the hope of an IPO.

The F1 Group planned an IPO on the Singapore Exchange in June 2012. The company was reportedly valued at $10 billion.

The listing did not materialise. Ecclestone cited the European financial crisis. However, Singapore's restriction on dual-class shares was a greater hurdle. Ecclestone was intent on maintaining his control of the F1 Group through two classes of shares. The investors in the IPO would subscribe to ordinary non-voting shares. Ecclestone would have the lion's share of the voting shares.

Last month, Singapore finally indicated that it may lift the restriction on dual-class shares. SGX's Listings Advisory Committee recommended dual-class shares. A dual-class share structure could draw marquee listings such as F1 and **Manchester United**. **Facebook**, **Alibaba Group Holding** and **Alphabet** have dual-class shares.

A listing by F1 and others of its standing could resuscitate Singapore's moribund equity market. There have been just six IPOs on the Mainboard this year. The largest of these, by IPO market capitalisation, was the listing of Malaysian glove maker **Top Glove Corp**. However, this was a secondary listing. Top Glove is also listed on Bursa Malaysia. The only other sizeable IPOs were those of **Frasers Logistics & Industrial Trust**, which raised $903 million; and **Manulife US REIT**, which raised US$470 million ($635.9 million).

Of the companies listed on SGX, more than half are trading below their book value and 7% below their net cash. The dire situation has led to stocks such as **OSIM International** being taken private.

Trading volumes have collapsed to a third of the level in 2006. Brokers are idling while waiting for the phone to ring. Some brokers such as **Standard Chartered** and **Barclays** have closed shop.

In *Weekend at Bernie's*, the two insurance executives went to immense lengths to raise Bernie from the dead. A listing of Bernie Ecclestone's empire would be just the tonic to revive the faltering Singapore market.

Postscript

The SGX is yet to attract a high profile listing due to its dual class structure. However, some tech companies like TikTok have moved their headquarters to Singapore, which may be a prelude to a listing.

Suppressing short-sellers is like shooting the messenger

Published on September 26, 2016

In Shakespeare's *Antony and Cleopatra*, the latter threatened to execute the messenger who informed her of Antony's marriage to Octavia. "I'll spurn thine eyes like balls before me! I'll unhair thy head!" she said while striking the hapless man.

Guangzhou-based Evergrande Real Estate Group (now known as **China Evergrande Group**) reacted in a similar way to a damning report issued by short-seller Andrew Left's Citron Research in 2012. The report alleged that Evergrande overstated its cash balance and exaggerated the value of its assets. It put the company's net gearing at 292%, well above the official 86%. The Hong Kong-listed shares of Evergrande promptly fell 20%.

Evergrande denied the claims in the Citron Research report and notified the police. It also complained to the Hong Kong Securities and Futures Commission, which appointed an investigative tribunal. Last month, the tribunal ruled that Left had engaged in market misconduct by publishing false or misleading data. It stated that Left was "reckless and negligent" in allowing Citron Research to publish the report on Evergrande. The penalties for this will be decided later, but Left may be required to forfeit his profits from shorting the stock.

The ruling is a body blow to short-sellers in this region. As it is, short-selling is restricted in several markets. With this ruling, short-sellers may avoid trumpeting their negative views, leaving the market with overwhelmingly adulatory research from brokerage firms. In Japan, for instance, more than 80% of stock calls are "buys".

Short-selling is a strategy commonly used by hedge funds. In fact, the founder of the world's first hedge fund did not hail from Wall Street. He was not even trained in finance, economics or business. Alfred Winslow Jones was a sociologist with degrees from Harvard and Columbia. He monitored civilian relief efforts for the Quakers in the Spanish Civil War and later wrote for *Fortune* magazine.

In 1949, at the ripe old age of 48, he founded the eponymous A.W. Jones & Co. Jones pioneered the use of leverage and shorting stocks to deliver better returns. A fund with $100,000 in capital that levers itself up to $130,000 and shorts $50,000 worth of stocks would have a net exposure to the market of only $80,000. Yet, this "hedged" fund would deliver a better return than if only $80,000 of the $100,000 in capital were invested.

Jones hired analysts to pick stocks, while he managed the firm. AW was a Jones that no one could keep up with. There are now more than 8,000 so-called hedge funds—rather than "hedged" funds—managing more than US$1 trillion ($1.3 trillion) in assets under management.

The hunger for short-selling ideas has created firms such as Left's Citron Research. Short-sellers are a vital force, as they provide liquidity, diversification and discipline.

Jim Chanos of Kynikos Associates, a diligent and determined short-seller, exposed the flaws in Enron's business model in October 2000, more than a year before its spectacular collapse. He questioned the company's use of mark-to-model accounting, as opposed to mark-to-market accounting. This approach vastly overstated earnings and artificially boosted its return on invested capital. Enron had also assembled a complex layer of off-balance sheet entities that camouflaged its frailties. In December 2001, the company filed for one of the largest bankruptcies in US history.

Citron Research's Left has not been as successful with his bet against Evergrande. Shares in the property company are now 39% higher than where they were just before Citron's report. The Hong Kong authorities have also found that Left acted improperly.

Yet, it would be a mistake to muffle short-sellers. While their negative views may not be independent, they are often just conveying uncomfortable facts. Just as stocks that are inflated eventually collapse, the fundamentals of stocks that are unfairly criticised eventually prevail. Let's not shoot the messenger for bringing us news that we detest. As Cleopatra's hapless messenger said, "Gracious madam, I that do bring the news made not the match."

Postscript

Short sellers have played a vital role in disciplining the market. Accounting frauds have been exposed. Luckin Coffee's fraudulent activity was exposed by Muddy Waters in early 2020.

Lessons from the Rumble in the Jungle

Published on June 20, 2016

Muhammad Ali's death has evoked tributes, with acres of newsprint devoted to his boxing as well as his opposition to the Vietnam War. But boxing and activism were not his only legacies.

Ali was the chief attraction in the definitive sporting event of his time—"the Rumble in the Jungle" in 1974. Ali faced George Foreman in Kinshasa, Zaire for the heavyweight championship of the world.

It was the first professional sporting event that was beamed to a worldwide TV audience. The sports coverage that we take for granted today—such as that of Formula One, Wimbledon and the English Premier League—had its roots in this bout.

The fight was conceived by Don King, an ambitious American promoter. He got former champion Ali and defending heavyweight champion Foreman to agree to a purse of US$5 million each (about US$24.3 million [$32.8 million] in today's terms) for a battle for the heavyweight title. King had a contract with the fighters, but he still needed a sponsor.

King found an unlikely sponsor in Zaire, now known as the Democratic Republic of Congo. Zaire was then ruled by President Mobutu Sese Seko, a dictator who governed with an iron fist. Mobutu saw an opportunity to raise publicity for Zaire by sponsoring the fight. US$10 million was a massive amount for a poor country, but Mobutu saw the commercial merits. It would immediately put his country on the map.

He was obsessive and image-conscious. In the prelude to the fight, the capital, Kinshasa, faced a crime wave. Mobutu rounded up 1,000 criminals and imprisoned them under the stadium that hosted the fight. One-tenth of the criminals were summarily executed. On the day of the fight, 50,000 spectators crammed into the stadium. The fight started at 4am to accommodate prime-time schedules in the US. Foreman was younger and stronger. He had a savage punch, which placed him as the favourite against an ageing Ali. His tenacity wore Foreman down and, in the eighth round, Ali knocked out Foreman.

Ali's punch was also a knockout blow for detractors of the business of sport. Satellite TV took sports coverage to an unprecedented scale. Fans from Greenland to New Zealand could follow a single sporting event. Sponsorship could be raised from global players. Although the fight was in Africa, top brands from the US such as Coke, Budweiser and McDonald's were lavish sponsors.

Televised sport became institutionalised with this event. In 1979, ESPN, a sports-focused cable channel, was launched. It acquired TV rights for baseball, basketball and American football. It branded itself as the "worldwide leader in sports". Cable TV vastly expanded the number of channels available on a TV set. It meant that ESPN could broadcast directly without dealing with local affiliates in the US or abroad.

The rise of the internet opened a new arena for sports broadcasts and gave fans greater flexibility. One could watch events at one's convenience. Also, a locally broadcast football game could be watched worldwide.

The internet provided ESPN with the icing on the cake. Its success is built on three pillars: First, it captures the broadcast rights for marquee sporting events such as Wimbledon and the Super Bowl for an extended period; second, it covers the cost through a range of lucrative sponsors; and third, it broadcasts it through a wide range of channels.

ESPN is a subsidiary of Disney, which is down 20% from its peak for the year. Investors are underestimating ESPN's enduring hold on world sports. More than half the earnings are driven by the sports subsidiary.

ESPN has widened its control of world sports. It has invested heavily in China, where basketball has become exceptionally popular. ESPN has partnered Chinese tech giant **Tencent Holdings** to provide basketball coverage to its one billion digital users. Disney's international subscribers have risen from 115 million to 127 million in the latest quarter; ESPN has a stranglehold on cricket in India. These investments suggest that ESPN's global subscriber base may grow even faster.

Just like how Muhammad Ali could adapt to his opponents' style, ESPN has proved to be durable. It is well set for the inevitable decline of cable. ESPN.com streams live sports content, which is viewed by 67 million unique visitors. A third of the entire time spent watching sports online is on this site.

Investors are likely to prosper by investing in sports broadcasting. They should remember that sweaty night in the heart of Africa. The eccentric tyrant and the famous fighters have left a legacy that has outlived them.

Postscript

Sports content has driven the stock performance of Disney and Tencent.

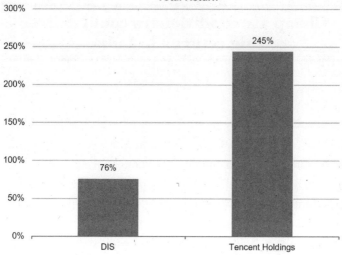

Cheap air conditioners could deliver big returns in India

Published on May 25, 2016

In 1986, I met a newspaper editor in Madras (now Chennai) who had air-conditioned the kennel of his Alsatians. Strangely, the kennel was the only part of his house that was air-conditioned. He explained that it kept the dogs passive. He valued their company more than that of humans.

Before the 1970s, the people who toiled in Singapore's offices and factories were less comfortable than this newspaper editor's dogs. Instead of air conditioners (ACs), most buildings here had ceiling fans at best. The heat and humidity wore one down. The stench of sweat engulfed factories. As ACs were installed in buildings over the next few decades, productivity improved. Today, even with temperatures soaring to nearly 40 degrees Centigrade, universal air-conditioning is keeping all of us comfortable indoors.

Singapore would be vastly different if not for Willis Carrier, inventor of the AC. In 1902, Carrier was a 25-year-old engineer working for a publishing company in Buffalo, New York. On a misty morning at a railway station, Carrier realised that he could dry air by passing it through water. By controlling humidity, the technological basis of modern air-conditioning was created. Carrier patented this process.

It took a few decades for ACs to take off, though. Until the 1950s, they were bulky and made a huge racket that drowned out conversation. With better technology, ACs became compact and quieter. Eventually, AC units that fit into a window to cool a single room were created, sparking huge demand. In 1948, about 74,000 ACs were sold in the US. Only six years later, more than a million ACs flew off the shelves. AC penetration in the tropics is more recent, but similarly meteoric. Today, more than 95% of Singapore homes have ACs, which is four times the level in 1990.

A similar inflection point for AC demand is looming. In the 1950s, the tipping point for the commercialisation of the AC was the compact design. But ACs are still only ubiquitous in the wealthy countries. They are relatively expensive and prodigious consumers of electricity. For instance, the US consumes more electricity

for cooling than Africa uses in total. In emerging Asian economies, most homes already have access to electricity, but only a fraction have ACs. In Indonesia, for instance, 75% of Indonesian homes have electricity, but only a 10th have ACs. The deterrent for these households is the unit cost of ACs and energy costs of maintenance.

Now, companies such as **Samsung** and **Whirlpool** have launched micro ACs priced at less than US$100 ($137) each. These ACs can be sold on a hire-purchase basis. A family with a monthly income of less than US$150 can pay just US$4 a month over two years. The other innovation is the rise of energy-efficient ACs such as the inverter, which reduces energy consumption by a third. Inverters are ideal in Africa, where power is expensive and unreliable. When people are able to afford ACs, demand will certainly accelerate. In China, for instance, AC penetration has risen from 8% in 1995 to more than 80% today.

Curiously, the market has yet to warm to the potential of AC producers. One counter that is heavily exposed to the cooling boom is Whirlpool India. The Indian subsidiary of the US appliance giant has a tight grip on India's AC market. AC penetration in India is below 5%, which is one-sixteenth of the level in China. Whirlpool India's operating earnings have tripled in the last four years. India also has an ambitious, home-grown AC producer—Symphony India, which is trading at a discount to Whirlpool India. Another fine proxy is Johnson Controls, a US company that expects to generate most of its growth from emerging markets.

Soon, a much larger proportion of Indians might be basking in the same cool comfort as the Alsatians I met in 1986. Investing in AC producers may be a fine way to benefit from it.

Postscript

India's craving for ACs has propelled Whirlpool stock price.

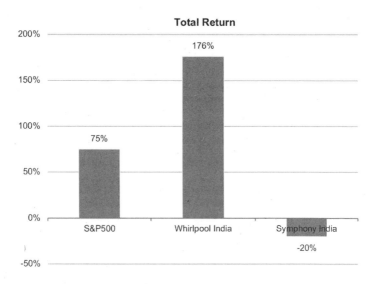

How Western Union and MoneyGram are making big money from small transfers

Published on February 29, 2016

In 2007, I flew to the Guyanese capital Georgetown for the Cricket World Cup. Though it is in South America, Guyana is considered part of the West Indies. I expected Georgetown to be a Caribbean delight with swaying palm trees on the sidewalks and piña coladas for breakfast.

Instead, I found a decaying and sterile town. The tallest building was just three storeys high. The Ministry of Education was the size of a Singapore shophouse. The streets were not lined with palm trees but with money transfer bureaus. The city may have more Western Union outlets per capita than any other in the world.

Guyana lives on foreign remittances. The former British colony has an English-speaking workforce that is dispersed in the UK, US and Canada. These overseas workers are employed as domestic helpers, cleaners, nurses and computer programmers. The country's 700,000 inhabitants are dwarfed by the one million strong Guyanese diaspora.

In 2015, Guyana received foreign remittances of US$438 million ($610.16 million), which is US$595 per capita and some 15% of its GDP. Guyana receives more in remittances than it earns through the export of rice, sugar and timber combined.

Guyana isn't the only country whose fortunes rest on foreign workers. Haiti is even more dependent on foreign remittances than Guyana. Without this income stream, these countries would face a balance of payments crisis.

Remittances cut poverty and boost consumption much more effectively than aid. When poor families receive remittances, they build houses and educate their children. In 2015, remittances to poor countries were US$440 billion, which was twice the foreign aid that these countries received. Unlike foreign aid, foreign remittances circumvent the corruption and bureaucracy of emerging markets.

Remitting money is not only a vast enterprise with an economic purpose, it is also lucrative business. The big daddy among the Money-Transfer Operators (MTOs) is NYSE-listed **Western Union**, which has a fifth of the global market.

Western Union was founded in 1851 as New York and Mississippi Valley Printing Telegraph Company. It was a pioneer in providing telegraph services. It adopted the name Western Union in 1856 and built the first transcontinental telegraph line in 1861.

Western Union's killer app was the use of communications technology for instant money transfer. In 1871, Western Union introduced money transfer that could be verified promptly through the telegraph. Over 145 years later, this innovation still forms the bedrock of this corporation's US$5.6 billion revenue.

Pioneering technology is not Western Union's sole asset. It has also built an awesome network of 500,000 agent locations in 200 countries. Western Union has increased the number of agents by fivefold in the last decade. Through this network, any one of the world's seven billion residents can send funds to another.

Western Union also has enormous pricing power and is immensely profitable. It boasts gross margins of 28% in most of the large markets. Western Union dictates prices according to location and the amount to be sent. For instance, to send US$200 from Dallas to Dhaka costs US$11. Sending the same amount from New York could cost US$21. In 2009, the G8 nations said they would aim to halve the global average cost of remitting funds from 10% in five years. Seven years later, the cost cuts are not even halfway there. It costs 7.7% on average to transfer money.

Despite the fat margins, the big banks are involved in less than 10% of this field. Banks avoid the money transfer field because their systems are built for the transfer of large amounts rather than the small sums that foreign workers transfer. Banks emphatically discourage small transfers by imposing charges on both sender and receiver.

Western Union has a few rivals, though. There is NASDAQ-listed **MoneyGram International**, which transfers about US$20 billion a year, and generates annual revenue of US$1.4 billion. There is another regional player in the Gulf called UAE Exchange, which is slightly larger than MoneyGram.

Xoom Corp is a feisty San Francisco-based upstart which charges a flat fee of US$5 per transaction. Most transactions are made from bank accounts. It handles about US$2 billion in revenue, but has grown rapidly. The rest of the market consists of small money-transfer agents and services such as **PayPal**.

Shares in Western Union and MoneyGram have tumbled because of the global meltdown. Western Union is down nearly 30% from its peak, while MoneyGram has collapsed 90%. But, the business model is sound and they are hard to dislodge. At nine times earnings, Western Union is trading at the bottom end of its price-to-earnings valuation band. The dominant MTO is also an income play with a dividend yield of 3.6%. MoneyGram is 5.7 times earnings, which is close to its all-time low. As I found on the streets of Georgetown in Guyana, there is big money in small transfers.

Postscript

Remittances have risen sharply. Western Union are MoneyGram are up, despite threats from disruptive rivals.

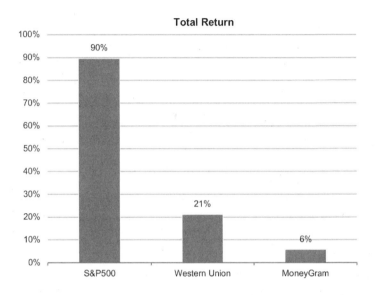

Event planning is a business set to thrive

Published on February 23, 2016

On Saturday, I attended the annual ball organized by the Oxbridge Society of Singapore at Eden Hall. The guests, many of whom travelled from overseas, wore black ties and ball gowns. The attendees were exceptionally diverse in terms of nationality, age and profession.

The guests sipped champagne, while they reminisced. The highlights were a stirring speech by Ms. Tan Su Shan of DBS and a piano recital by Ms. Ksheniia Vokhmianina, a Ukrainian maestro.

Several guests complained bitterly about digital disruption. A stockbroker said that online trading was a dark cloud on his industry. Brokerage commissions were a quarter of the level in 1996. A surgeon worried about robots making him obsolete. A patents lawyer spoke of cheaper and nimbler rivals in Bangalore.

The fear of digital disruption would imply that events such as the Oxbridge ball were doomed. In the age of Skype and WhatsApp, there is less of a compulsion for face-to-face meetings. People could listen to the piano recital through Spotify.

In fact, conferences and gala dinners are blossoming. Singapore is facing conference hyperinflation. In the equities industry, there is a major conference every month. Each event promises celebrities like Tony Blair and Madonna, as well as "networking opportunities".

Singapore has long eliminated rodents as a health scare, but the tourism industry is driven by MICE. MICE stands for meetings, incentive travel, conferences and entertainment. Singapore's value of the MICE industry has grown at a CAGR of 7% in the last decade, which is much higher than the GDP growth. The US$18 billion tourism sector is dependent on conferences and conventions.

On the international scene, the jewel in the crown of conferences takes place in the icy resort of Davos in Switzerland. Every January, the world's business and political elite jostle for places at the World Economic Forum (WEF).

Davos symbolizes the pull of conferences. This year 2,500 guests from 100 countries spent four days in Davos. The delegates were undeterred by the plunging stock markets and commodity collapse.

It costs SF 600,000 a year for a company to be a strategic partner. The conference generated SF200 million in revenue, which is a 40% increase from the 2011 figure. The mountains of Switzerland have a long way to go to peak as a conference venue.

What is driving the stampede for these events? Perhaps, internet fatigue has set in. People spend so much time on digital communication that the real-life alternative is a welcome respite. Having a coffee with a conference delegate is far superior to Facebook chat.

Also, a conference creates the setting for chance encounters. One can bump into a potential client in the hallway. Business ventures can be hatched in the bar. Internet communication is so commoditized that people have become weary.

There are some tasks that can only be done in person. Despite the vast advances of the Internet, we have not figured out a way to backslap on it.

A final function of conferences is an evolutionary one — tribalism. We all want to be part of an exclusive group.

The best way to play the event explosion may be under

our noses in Singapore. Singapore has 31 listed REITs, six of them are hospitality REITs. The hospitality REITs own and operate hospitality properties such as hotels and serviced apartments. They are proxies for Singapore's relentless march as the event capital of world.

There are a couple of factors that investors should realise about the hospitality REITs. Tourist arrivals can be volatile on a quarterly basis. For instance, last year's Rupiah collapse cut Indonesian arrivals. In 2003, SARs was a sharp and short blow to the MICE industry. Hence, the REITs that have a higher portion of their revenue from fixed leases as opposed to variable leases are likely to weather the storm.

Second, REITs have varying degrees of debt. The interest coverage ratio ranges from 9x to 4x. But, the vital factor is the level of the fixed interest payments that they have. Last year saw the Fed raise rates for the first time in a decade. **Ascott Residence Trust** has 70% of its debt on a fixed rate basis, despite a low interest coverage ratio of 4x. They can weather an interest rate hike better than most.

One of the diners at the Oxbridge event was ruminating on the best career path for her son. She was torn between urging him to be a lawyer or a surgeon. I told her to encourage him to be an event planner. That profession is likely to be thriving when Oxford University celebrates its thousandth anniversary in 2096!

Postscript

CDL Hospitality Trust has not delivered strong returns. It has fallen victim to the pandemic, as conferences have been wiped out. If the vaccine takes effect, it may well be a leader of the recovery.

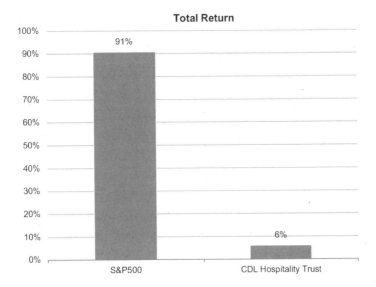

Total Return

European defence stocks may blossom

Published on November 23, 2015

Friedrich Nietzsche wrote that if you want to fight with dragons, you have to become one. Nietzsche died in 1900, but he could be describing the West's response to terrorism in 2015.

The devastating bombings in Paris last Friday were followed by swift retribution by the French military. The country's response to the tragedy has been a familiar one. Arbitrary arrests, detention without trial and expulsion of foreigners have begun in earnest. The French bombardment of Syria has satisfied a visceral urge for revenge. There are now fears of European military engagement in the Middle East.

The attacks on the World Trade Center's twin towers on Sept 11, 2001 were an atrocity that has few parallels in the long history of evil. They were followed by the same measures— derided by civil libertarians—that France is embarking on. America's post-9/11 defence industry consolidation provides vital lessons for Europe's defence industry.

While civil libertarians condemned the US response to terrorism, it was a godsend to the American defence industry. The last 14 years have been bountiful for US defence companies. Defence spending has had a massive impact on the stock performance of America's largest firms. These include the Big Five: Lockheed Martin, Boeing, Northrop Grumman, Raytheon and General Dynamics.

Sept 11 took place while the defence industry was struggling. The 1990s had been particularly trying. It was a time of peace. The end of the Cold War limited business opportunities. Defence companies consolidated in the face of contraction. The industry coalesced around these five players. The US defence budget has doubled in inflation-adjusted terms from US$304 billion in 2000 to US$637 billion ($907 billion) in 2015. Defence spending peaked at US$717 billion in 2011. The death of Osama bin Laden in 2011 led to defence budget cuts.

Despite these budget cuts, the US is the largest spender on defence by a wide margin. In 2001, the US share of the world defence spending was 35%. Today, the proportion is 43%.

The five defence companies prospered almost by default. By remaining in the field, they were beneficiaries of the government's defence largesse. US$1 invested in these five "defence diamonds" on Sept 10, 2001 would be worth US$6.30 today. These stocks outperformed the Standard & Poor's 500 by more than 350 percentage points. US$1 invested in the S&P 500 is worth US$2.55 today.

Defence stocks, along with aerospace stocks, are safe investments during conflicts. These companies have consistent earnings due to government contracts. The cash flow can be unpredictable, as receivables can be high. But revenue is typically reliable in this belligerent world. Also, the collection risks in the industry are minimal, as the principal customers are governments.

There is a strange symmetry between the Paris attacks and 9/11. The European industry is facing the same travails that the US defence sector was grappling with in 2001. The European financial crisis has led to a drop in EU spending from €200 billion in 2008 to less than €160 billion ($242 billion) in 2014. Europe's defence industry is divided along national lines. Since the euro crisis arose in 2011, the defence companies have been facing spiralling costs, excess capacity and chronic budget cuts. According to IHS Jane's, an intelligence organisation, the European overcapacity in combat aircraft, land vehicles and naval shipbuilding may be as high as 30%.

The adversity led to talk of consolidation among the European defence contractors. In 2012, Europe's largest aerospace firm, EADS, tried to merge with the continent's biggest defence firm, BAE Systems. The move did not succeed, owing to regulatory pressure, but smaller firms consolidated. The rationale is that consolidation would create substantial cost savings in R&D. Marketing is another area of synergy.

In an eerie echo of September 2001, the European defence industry is dominated by a handful of players. Apart from BAE Systems and EADS, the leaders include Airbus Group, Safran and Thales. It is likely that defence spending could rise sharply in the EU in the wake of the Paris bombings. Investors should keep an eye out for these companies.

Europe's defence spending is about a third that of the US. However, the domestic industry gets complete priority in EU defence contracts. The recent terrorist attacks in France would lead to greater allocation for military and surveillance operations.

European defence firms are also prominent in the US. BAE Systems competes with Boeing, Lockheed Martin and others for Pentagon contracts.

The **STOXX Europe TMI Aerospace & Defence Index** comprises the top 15 firms in the industry. The index has almost doubled in the past five years in euro currency terms. But, investing in the sector may be an ideal response to the vicious dragon of terrorism.

Postscript

The European defence stocks have been defensive investments.

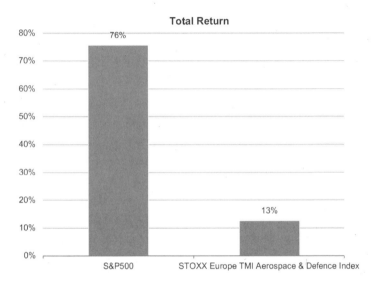

Total Return

Long March of chicken in Asia

Published on August 4, 2015

In 1983, the world was swinging to the tune of Michael Jackson's *Thriller*. The *Thriller* is no longer top of the pops, but a culinary novelty that was introduced in 1983 is about to thrill Asia. The Chicken McNugget was launched by McDonald's in that year. It transformed chicken from a product sold in its raw form to a processed, consumer product.

The rise of the chicken nugget owes much to the tenacity of Don Tyson, then CEO of Tyson Foods, one of the world's largest chicken producers. Tyson Foods was founded by Don Tyson's father in Springdale, Arkansas, a rural backwater. Don Tyson's mild manner belied a titanic drive. He had lobbied McDonald's for 14 years before the vast restaurant chain finally agreed to introduce chicken nuggets in 1983. Tyson Foods was the principal supplier.

Don Tyson was one of the first to see the transformative potential of processed chicken, especially the nugget. It would liberate chicken from the volatility of raw material pricing. Consumers would be drawn to the ease of eating the neat and compact nuggets.

The Chicken McNugget heralded a revolution in America's industry. Chicken began to be sold in a more ready-to-eat format. The sale of whole birds made way for more processed and cut-up chicken. In 1983, only 14% of America's chicken was sold in processed form. Today, it is over 75%.

The advent of processed chicken has insulated meat giants such as Tyson Foods, Pilgrim's Pride and Sanderson Farms from the fluctuations in chicken prices. Comparing Tyson

Food's chicken operating margins against the price of chicken reveals immunity from fluctuations.

Processed chicken products such as McNuggets were a killer app for chicken. In 1992, nine years after the launch of the McNugget, chicken overtook beef to become the most consumed meat. In 2012, per capita chicken consumption in the US stood at 85 pounds, twice that of beef.

There is a strange symmetry between the US meat market in 1983 and ASEAN in 2015. The ratio of processed chicken to overall chicken consumption in ASEAN today is similar to the level in the US in 1983.

The ASEAN economies are mostly emerging societies, on the cusp of prosperity. Rising prosperity leads to higher meat consumption. It also accelerates once an economy reaches a certain threshold. The middle-income threshold (defined by the World Bank as USD 2,000) is one point where the acceleration starts. From the USD2,000 per capita GDP threshold, meat consumption growth matches GDP growth. Once a country crosses the USD5,000 threshold, meat consumption growth is in excess of GDP growth. Indonesia has crossed the per capita GDP inflection point of USD2,000, while China has crossed the USD5,000 threshold.

Chicken is intensely relevant to emerging markets as it is the cheapest form of animal protein. The amount of feed required to produce one kg of chicken meat is just 2kg. The corresponding figure for pork and beef is up to four times as high.

Chicken is not just the cheapest meat, its lead time is lower than that of pork and beef. This is a vital advantage in a volatile commodity market.

ASEAN is fertile ground for chicken. Indonesia is the most populous Muslim country in the world and the largest market for Halal products. Halal is the term used for food that is permissible under Muslim law. Examples of permissible animals are chickens, cows, sheep and goats. Avian meat, like chicken or duck, must not have fed on avian meat.

Halal consciousness is rising in Indonesia. Chicken has been identified as a Halal-compliant product. The global Halal food and beverage market was worth an estimated USD1.1 trillion in 2013. Most of it is centred on products such as chicken.

Charoen Pokphand Foods is Asia's answer to Tyson Foods. It has a vice-like grip on Asia's meat market. It is following Tyson Food's trajectory by adopting the modern operational techniques such as mechanized slaughter farms. Vertical integration is another Tyson feature that they have adopted. Feed farms, DOC breeding and raw chicken are occurring under a single roof.

Processed chicken, however, is at a nascent stage in ASEAN. Less than a fifth of the revenue of the listed chicken companies is from processed chicken.

ASEAN is now facing a Chicken McNugget moment. Change is in the air. The leading chicken players could devote a third of their capital expenditure to adapting the chicken nugget to the Asian palette. Dishes such as Chicken Mee Goreng are being packaged in an accessible form. Processed chicken share of the chicken market could rise sharply, driving profits with it.

"There's no escaping the jaws…" said Michael Jackson in *Thriller*. If he was referring to the jaws of this region's protein hungry, there may be a nugget of truth to it.

Postscript

The chicken producers have flown. As the cheapest form of protein, they remain as a shining example of consumer growth in Asia.

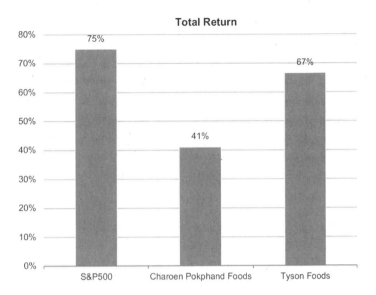

Total Return

Fridges may heat up consumer stocks

Published on July 22, 2015

The ASEAN consumer market is on the cusp of profound change due to a simple home appliance – the fridge.

Barely noticed by investors, fridges are potentially as transformative of consumer behaviour as cars were to transport. Without fridges, milk and chicken would have to be consumed almost immediately. Corned beef and yoghurt would be unheard of. Now, the proliferation of fridges in homes across countries like Indonesia, Thailand and Vietnam is quietly reshaping consumption patterns and fuelling the growth of the region's food and beverage groups.

Fridges partly owe their existence to Frederic Tudor, a 19th century American merchant. He was born to an erudite Boston family, but commerce was his calling. He was known as the "Ice King" for his overwhelming passion to make ice commercially viable. In the early 1800s, ice was quite simply harvested where it existed and transported as quickly as possible to where there was demand. Not surprisingly, it was an obscure product, unknown in many parts of the West.

In the 1830s, Tudor founded the Wenham Lake Ice Company, which became a pioneer in transporting ice to England. His first shipment confounded British customs officials. They did not know how to classify the ice. All three hundred tonnes melted while the officials deliberated on the classification. Tudor also met resistance from ship owners who feared that the frozen water might sink their vessels if it melted.

Yet, Tudor had icy determination. He spearheaded technological advances that allowed ice to travel from Boston to Bombay. After suffering years of losses and derision, ice finally caught on. By the 1850s, ice was America's largest export in terms of weight. Ice became a hot item in American households too. By 1865, two-thirds of Boston households had ice delivered daily. A range of novelties such as chilled beer and ice cream appeared.

Ice took on a life of its own with another innovation – refrigerated railway cars. This masterstroke also allowed perishables such as meat to travel the breadth of the United States. In 1913, refrigerators for home use were invented. And, as electricity spread, fridges gradually became the ubiquitous home appliance that we know today.

Yet, in many emerging economies, fridges are still beyond the reach of many people. In Indonesia, for instance, only a fourth of households have one. That's despite electricity penetration of 73%. It seems that affordability, not access to the electricity grid, is the barrier to fridge penetration.

A typical fridge costing US$100-120, is a third of the average monthly income in Indonesia. The average wage is US$9 a day. However, this figure masks stark inequalities. Almost four-fifths of Indonesians live on less than US$4 a day (US$120 a month). So, in reality, a typical fridge costs roughly an entire month's income.

This hurdle is about to be crossed as fridge manufacturers look to sell smaller cooling units targeting the poor. LG Electronics, for instance, is now selling small fridges priced at US$50-60 a unit. The capacity of the fridge is more than sufficient for the meat, milk and soft drink requirements of lower income customers.

This could quickly spark a change in consumption patterns and create opportunities for food companies. For instance, chicken is mostly sold in its raw form in the region. Processed chicken, which requires refrigeration, accounts for only one-fifth of the chicken consumed. With fridges in the homes of consumers, this could change. Chicken producers such as Charoen Pokphand Foods, Charoen Pokphand Indonesia and Japfa Comfeed plan to devote a major slice of their capex to processed chicken.

Similarly, Indonesia's per capita milk consumption is currently only 15 litres a year, which is less than half the per capita consumption in China, Singapore and Thailand. Milk is also overwhelmingly sold in powdered or UHT form, which doesn't require refrigeration. Indofood Consumer Branded Products, Ultrajaya and Unilever Indonesia have noted a craving for fresh milk. In Vietnam, where Fraser & Neave is active through its stake in Vinamilk, fresh milk use could rise sharply.

Then, there are soft drinks, which are best drunk chilled in the tropics. As more households acquire fridges, more soft drinks are likely to be consumed at home. Indofood CBP is preparing for the onset of fridges with a joint venture with Asahi of Japan to produce soft drinks. The aim is to combine Indofood CBP's distribution network and Asahi's soft drinks expertise.

Frederic Tudor's efforts to popularise ice in New England in the 19th century might be about to heat up the ASEAN consumer market in the 21st century.

Postscript

The beneficiaries of the fridge boon have been red hot. We are still at a nascent stage, as half the households in emerging Asia do not have fridges.

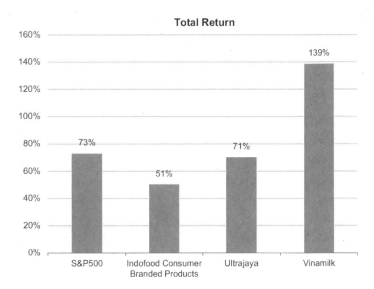

Can we escape the ghosts of 1997?

Published on June 23, 2015

On 2 July, I was slated to appear on CNBC at 6.45am to talk about emerging markets. However, due to a series of mishaps, including a taxi that didn't appear and an absent security guard, I failed to make it to the studio on time. Instead, I was interviewed over the phone as I paced the SGX lobby while viewers looked at an airbrushed photograph of me. I felt embarrassed and couldn't help whether the ghosts of Asia's financial crisis 18 years ago might be haunting me.

It was on 2 July 1997 that the Thai Baht depreciated sharply from 24.4 per US dollar to 29.15. The Thai government could no longer support its US dollar peg. The contagion quickly spread, with currencies and asset markets in Southeast Asia collapsing. Even South Korea, Japan and Hong Kong were not spared. India and China, who were then isolated, were the only major Asian economies that were unscathed.

The disruption and devastation was massive. Indonesia was the worst hit. By January 1998, the rupiah had depreciated some 87% versus the US dollar. In US dollar terms, the total market capitalisation of its listed companies had shrunk to less than 7% of their July 1997 level. On the same basis, many other Asian markets had fallen to a third of their July 1997 levels. The loss of wealth was the most precipitous since the 1929 Wall Street crash.

The crisis was rooted in the flood of hot money that had entered the region since the 1980s. In 1997, Thailand, Indonesia and South Korea had large current account deficits. Virtually fixed exchange rates encouraged excessive external borrowing. Steady Safe, an Indonesian taxi company, had over US$265 million in foreign debt, despite all its revenue being denominated in rupiah. The economies were severely exposed to foreign exchange risk.

In early 1997, a US rate hike effectively pricked the bubble. Exports, the main driver of Asian growth, were already flagging. Portfolio investment retreated from the region.

Yet, the recovery from the crisis was as dramatic as the collapse. With the steep fall in their currencies, Asia's economies suddenly became much more competitive exporters. In fact, by 1998, many economies in the region were running current account surpluses. And, by 2011, Indonesia's market capitalisation returned to its 1997 peak in US dollar terms.

Today, Asia's markets are much safer and robust. Economic reforms have taken root since 1997. Bank balance sheets are more secure. Non-performing loans ratios are now below 10%, compared to almost 50% in 1997. There are also restrictions on US dollar borrowing in unproductive sectors. Most Asian economies are also running current account surpluses.

Yet, the ominous parallels with 1997 are hard to ignore. A US rate hike seems likely after seven years of low interest rates. Currencies across the ASEAN region have fallen sharply this year. The rupiah, for instance, is down 14% in the last year. The ringgit is down 16%, breaching 3.8 versus the US dollar, which is the level at which it was pegged in 1998.

So, what should investors do? Is there opportunity once more amid the slump in the region's currencies? Palm oil, a commodity that is the bedrock of ASEAN's prosperity, could be an answer. Indonesia and Malaysia produce 85% of the world's palm oil supply. Plantation companies operating in these two countries are benefitting from their weakening currencies. Their costs are in rupiah and ringgit while crude palm oil (CPO) is denoted in US dollars.

As it happens, the El Niño weather phenomenon, which ravaged the region in 1983, 1997, 2006 and 2010, is affecting palm oil productivity again. That could drive up palm oil prices, further boosting the margins of the plantations. Meteorologists are expecting the most intense El Niño weather pattern since 1997 this year.

One palm oil stock that stands out in the local market is **Golden Agri-Resources**. It has a hectarage that is seven times Singapore's land mass. Its earnings are 85% correlated to CPO prices. Other palm oil stocks in Singapore include **Indofood Agri** and **First Resources**, which are also Indonesian based.

Currency shocks like 1997 can be nasty and brutish. And, it seems that even a meticulously planned TV appearance can be waylaid by its ghosts. Yet, investors who remember what happened might be able to position themselves if history repeats.

Postscript
ASEAN has averted another 1997 currency crisis. The economies have better current accounts and balance sheets.

Acknowledgements

This book would not be possible without the encouragement of friends and colleagues.

PN Balji, former editor of the *Today*, introduced me to Marshall Cavendish. I am forever in his debt.

The articles first appeared in my column in *The Edge*. The management of that esteemed publication deserve credit for their dedication. Bernard Tong and Chan Chao Peh, as well as its previous editors BK Tan, Ben Paul and Michelle Teo have backed my work. Assif Shameen and Manu Bhaskaran first connected me to *The Edge* in 2004.

My former senior colleagues have expanded my horizons. These include Arjuna Mahendran, Richard Pell-Ilderton, Faizal Syed, Joe Batchelor, Dave Murray, Peter Hilton, Adrian Foulger, Benedict Perez, Arthur Pineda, Regina Lim, Nilesh Jasani, Nita Halim, Chris Holland, Sutha Kandiah, Muzahir Degani, Venkatesh Sethuraman, Elena Yoon, Nilesh Jasani and Anand Kumar.

My employer Tellimer is on the ascendancy. I thank Duncan Wales, Hasnain Malik, Rahul Shah, Ian Hamilton, Ian Watts, Bansi Jashapara, Nick Beazley and Igor Chernomorskiy for their steadfast support.

Fund managers consume my recommendations. Their in-sights have improved my understanding. These include David Halpert, Tim Campbell, Graham Muirhead, James Johnstone, Vishal Sharma, Sandeep Dhingra, Nudgem Richyal, Amit Bhartia, Murali Srikantaiah, Randy Cheung, Tom Grant, Samir Arora, Ricky Liew, Namit Nayegandhi, Andrew Mattock, Rashmi Kwatra, Salman Niaz, Jasjit Rekhi and John Foo.

My friends have indulged my writing. These include Mike Marqusee, Steve Diggle, Ian Roberts, Satish Selvanathan, Anjhula Mya Bais, N Ram, Anurag Das, Shekhar Gupta, Ramachandra Guha, Kelly Yang, Angela Clark, Faith Thoms, Kathy O'Brien, Jahnavi Bhagwati, Chandi Jayawickrama, Eroy Basnayake, Shivani Chander Das, Neel Chowdhury, Mark Matthews, PK Basu, Alex Lovell, Krishan Balendra, Rahul Anand, Pradeep Maharaja, Jean Nabaa, Thirukumar Nadesan, Sanjeev Sanyal, Kiran Vadlamani, Lena Mukhey, Clarence Dias, Tobias Hoschka and Amit Sibal.

Other friends have supported me through thick and thin. These are Reshani Dangalle, Vinay Ganga, Soraya Cader, Liron Lev, Jeanette Mertz, Navin Dissanayake, Rashmin Lokubandara, Eroy Basnayake, Shobi Cooke, Naaila Francis, Sabreena Andriesz, Galina Gusarevich, Sharada Selvanathan, Leena Hirdaramani, R Rajamahendran, Dinah Haji-Omar, Suhasini Haidar, Himraj Dang, Anisha Mohinani, Vinod Hirdaramani, Tushar Pathak, Sarath Sathkumara, Ashwin Ranganathan and Nimal Cooke.

My Teachers have guided and chided my work. They include Sita Nayar, Bernd Pflug, Adam Pleasance, Laddie Ponniah, Gowher Rizvi and Michael Freeden.

The media have aired my views. Sri Jegarajah, Lisa Oake, Oriel Morrison, Penny Chen, Karishma Vaswani, May Kek, Desley Humphrey, Anand Menon, Marianne Star Inacay, Netty Ismail, Steve Gwynn-Jones, Caroline Ng, Zarina Hussain, Josie Ling, Abhishek Vishnoi, Yoolim Lee, Netty Ismail, Ishika Mookerjee, Rachel Kelly and Manus Cranny.

Melvin Neo of Marshall Cavendish took the book to the finish line.

About the Author

Nirgunan Tiruchelvam is a Singaporean equity analyst. He has worked for Standard Chartered, ABN Amro and RBS. He is now an equity analyst with Tellimer (formerly Exotix Partners).

Nirgunan is a graduate of Oxford University and has written for *The Edge* and the *Financial Times*. He has appeared as a TV commentator on BBC, Channel News Asia, CNBC and Bloomberg. His views have been cited by the *Wall Street Journal* and Reuters.

Index